THE
CONNECTORS

THE CONNECTORS

How the World's Most
Successful Businesspeople
Build Relationships and
Win Clients for Life

MARIBETH KUZMESKI

WILEY

JOHN WILEY & SONS, INC.

Published by John Wiley & Sons, Inc., Hoboken, New Jersey
Published simultaneously in Canada

For general information on our other products and services or for technical support, please contact our Customer Care Department within the United States at (800) 762-2974, outside the United States at (317) 572-3993 or fax (317) 572-4002.

Wiley also publishes its books in a variety of electronic formats. Some content that appears in print may not be available in electronic books. For more information about Wiley products, visit our web site at www.wiley.com.

ISBN: 978-0470-48818-8 (cloth)

Printed in the United States of America.

10 9 8 7 6 5 4 3 2

CONTENTS

To my family, my clients, and my friends who have taught me to be a better connector.
Aclyio!

INTRODUCTION

They may forget what you said, but they will never forget how you made them feel.
> —Carl W. Buehner (1898-1974), Mormon leader,
> businessman, and author

I have the great fortune of being able to personally meet some of the most successful sales professionals in the world—some of whom we work with at my marketing consulting firm. I have been long captivated with the "how do they do it" aspect of success in business, as many of us of course are. How do they think? What are their characteristics? What are the similarities among the most successful businesspeople? What consistent actions do they take? What drives them? What has combusted to make them who they are and to produce such exceptional accomplishments?

Interestingly, this same curiosity about what makes others successful is also present in those enjoying current success. The individuals and firms with whom we consult know that we have other profitable businesses with whom we work with on strategy and business development. That is the reason, I believe, that the most frequently asked questions I hear are "What are other firms doing that's working?" or "What exactly is she doing to bring on so many sales?"

As businesspeople, many of us have a great desire to continue to get better and better, and not get caught being stagnant or too comfortable in our current situation. And, if we can find out what someone else has taken the time to discover and use with success, perhaps we can learn from that and not make mistakes which others have already made and corrected. But if simply knowing and implementing successful tactics in practice by others is the secret to success, then you would think that each proven idea, sales tactic, marketing strategy, or business system would be taken by the masses and turned into extraordinary sales. However, we know that's not how it works.

Therefore, the most profitable businesses and individuals in the world must possess something *unique*. I have spent a lot of time considering their intellectual power, their competitiveness, their determination, their implementation strategies, their staff, their funding options, and just about anything else you can think of that may distinctively contribute to such positive results. When we break down the characteristics that extraordinary businesspeople do possess, much of them are what we may consider to be some of the obvious enviable traits: persistence, drive, hard work, intelligence, ability to generate new ideas, ability to change, a "Never take no for an answer" mindset, and so on.

However, there is one more key characteristic, and it is these individuals' particular ability to connect with others and form meaningful relationships.

This is not as simple as academic intelligence or an entrepreneurial spirit. The ability to connect is a different kind of intelligence, one that is the proverbial icing on the cake for most of the people who have reached to high levels of greatness. And without the icing, the cake probably can't be an incredibly delectable cake; it would be missing a key ingredient. The cake alone may be delicious, but it really only becomes an extraordinary cake with the icing to top it off—assuming it is the right amount and taste of the perfect icing.

This ability to connect with others is indeed the icing on the cake. Relating in an impactful way brings sales, leadership power, and personal success. It is an innate skill in some, but something that everyone can learn and improve upon. Yet it is truly a secret to success because it is often dismissed. We have a tendency to brush off the importance our ability to connect and create relationships is as a key contributor and explanation for business success.

True connections need to be made with feeling and purpose and honesty. I know because I watch my clients do it every day. I have also spent a great deal of time, research, and energy on working through this very concept myself, applying it in my life, and continuing to work and learn at this most critical element in success. It is something I will always work at and, hopefully, continue to get better at. It is a constant process.

Unfortunately, our ability to connect can be lost in a fraction of the amount of time that it took us to develop it. It seems sometimes that just one setback in our career or plan and—whomp!—we are back to the old "me, me, me" attitude that leaves little room for concern for others. But staying true to others and making a real effort to connect with them will no doubt make their lives better and ours too. Cultivating relationships undoubtedly leads to success in just about anything that we do. And it is a skill that must be practiced and trained.

The first experience that I had that really differentiated these characteristics of success took place while I was working with a financial advisor and his firm. We were hired to help them improve their marketing strategies and bring on new clients. The principle in the firm, Roch Tranel, measured progress by the amount of client assets they brought under their management at the firm. His goal was to grow into a large financial services firm with hundreds of millions in money under management.

Since I had not worked with a financial services firm prior to this (and thanks to this client, we now we work with hundreds of financial firms each year!), I started by looking at the opportunities that existed and the type of prospecting that may work for attracting clients who would invest their savings with this firm. I asked Tranel how he had acquired clients in the past. Much of his success, interestingly, was rooted in his fear of prospecting. He didn't want to cold call or employ similar strategies. So, he just kept calling and talking with those who had already done business with his firm. He kept himself busy by avoiding the typical prospecting strategies of reaching people who didn't know him.

The result was unintentional but amazing: His handful of clients *truly* loved him. They cared about his success; they brought him food; they sent birthday cards to his wife and his growing family of kids. And a valuable by-product of this was a stream of referrals. Tranel was only in his 20s, and he had little experience. But because of his drive and determination to stay in business and communicate properly with his few clients, they began to genuinely like and trust him. As a result, his few clients began recommending him to others who worked at the same company.

When I began working for his firm, I knew that prospecting for people that had no connection to Roch Tranel was going to be a long shot based on his propensity for prospecting. So, we simply took his model of communicating and acquiring referrals and made a system out of it. His strength was connecting with others; he just needed to do it more systematically and to more people. And, his staff needed to do the same thing.

Today, The Tranel Financial Group is one of the top financial firms in the United States. They do manage hundreds of millions in client assets. Roch Tranel has given my firm much credit for his quick ascent to success. But in reality, his ability to connect was the one great strength. We built an entire marketing system around that ability and then transferred that ability and connection techniques to his staff, and it multiplied and multiplied.

Is it possible to build an entire, multimillion-dollar business around your ability to connect? It seems so. And it is the best way to build a business effectively, efficiently, profitably, and quickly.

Others firms have seen the kind of success that Roch Tranel and his firm have enjoyed. They have asked me to do just what Roch did in his firm—build a model around the acquisition of referrals. And the model that I have developed is as follows:

1. Delight Clients
2. Acquire Referrals
3. Invite Referrals to Educational Workshops
4. Acquire Clients
5. Repeat Process from #1.

It is actually a very uncomplicated strategy. Systematize your operation around your clients, build niches of clients, put on educational workshops, convert clients, and repeat. We've employed this system with great success in many firms. However, it is not as easily executed as it may appear to be. The key is the very first step: delighted clients. How you get to having a delighted client is much more complex than just sending them a few letters and visiting with them once a year to go over their accounts. It is a process that begins with the learned and cultivated ability to connect.

Connecting with others is not incredibly difficult. But if it were easy, then wouldn't you think that more people would take the time to work harder at connecting with others and developing deeper relationships? It may be that our trust issues or a habit of focus does not necessarily include others. Many businesspeople have established a survival-of-the-fittest-type attitude.

My purpose in writing this book is to share with you what some of the most successful people have done to create better relationships and to show you how this has been the missing link in attempts to be more successful, bring on more new business, and create the kind of client loyalty that will win clients for life. Connecting at a deeper level can be achieved without spending money on consultants, courses, marketing strategies, psychologists, or spiritual consultants. It simply requires that you focus on others and have a plan to serve them, pay attention to them, listen to them, and care about them.

Our research and findings describe what has given successful businesspeople—some you will recognize and others you probably won't—the ability to reach higher levels of achievement than most. Their stories and the principles they use to connect with others—resulting in unique business accomplishments—fill the pages of this book. It is not their business acumen alone that has brought them to positions of such prominence. The key determinant at the top of all business strategies, talents, and expertise is the ability to connect with people on a meaningful level—one that produces quality associations and profitable business relationships.

In essence, it is how we make others feel within the connections that we have that brings the success we desire.

Winning Business with Relationships

The Common Denominator of Greatness and Success

It's Not Money, It's People!

We cannot live only for ourselves. A thousand fibers connect us with our fellow men; and among those fibers, as sympathetic threads, our actions run as causes, and they come back to us as effects.

—Herman Melville

Great! It's a word we hear and use often: "Great game!" "Great shot!" "Great work!" "Great movie!" "Great song!" "Great party!" "Great _____ (fill in the blank)!"

"How are you feeling today?"

"Great!"

"What great weather we're having."

"The food at that new restaurant in town is great."

"We had a great time last night."

And the beat goes on! We use the word "great" in referring to amount, extent, scope, exceptional or praiseworthy accomplishment or performance, or someone who's widely known and esteemed. The late comedian and actor Jackie Gleason was called "The Great One," as is former National Hockey League star Wayne Gretzky.

In boxing, being known merely as great wasn't quite good enough for former Olympic gold medalist and heavyweight champion Muhammad Ali. Never the shy and retiring type, Ali would frequently proclaim himself "The Greatest," a name his fans quickly adopted in referring to him. On one occasion, however, he said, "I'm not the greatest," but immediately followed that seemingly humble remark by declaring, "I'm the double greatest."

In addition to having "great" or "greatest" attached to their names, Gleason, Gretzky, and Ali were certainly very successful in their chosen pursuits, but does that necessarily suggest a correlation between greatness and success? Is every great person successful, and every successful person great? Hardly!

We have great-aunts, great-uncles and great-grandparents, who may or may not always be as great as those names suggest. Nor is "great" always used to describe people. Australia, for example, has its Great Barrier Reef, China its Great Wall, and the United States its Great Lakes and Great Smoky Mountains. And while the word "great" is most often attached to something positive, it can also have negative connotations, as in "The Great Plague" and "The Great Depression."

So, given the frequency with which we apply the word "great" in so many different ways, how do we go about defining greatness? How can we measure or recognize when it's been achieved? And what's the connection between greatness and success?

Secrets of Greatness

In 2006, *Fortune* magazine published a three-part series titled "Secrets of Greatness." The first part, titled "How I Work," appeared in its March 20 issue and included interviews with a dozen men and women labeled "super achievers," representing various segments of the business and professional spectrum. All these super achievers—most of them quite well known—have been very prosperous in their chosen fields, and so the magazine's writers set out to find the reasons for their success.

Not surprisingly, most of them get up early and stay up late, getting by on four to six hours of sleep. Proper diet and exercise are also mentioned frequently. Most rely heavily on technology to keep up; for a few, the gadgets are limited to their cell phones. Some are good at multitasking, while others like time alone to think—one does so by standing on his head. Some credit delegation as a key to their success, and for others it's maintaining a strict to-do list.

The second in the "Secrets of Greatness" series (June 12, 2006) was titled "Teamwork," and it described how some teams achieved great success, while others failed miserably. In the introductory article, *Fortune* magazine writer Jerry Useem warned that "The fact is, most of what you read about teamwork is bunk," and what follows are several examples that prove his point.

One of his examples was the 2004 U.S. Men's Olympic Basketball Team. Prior to that time, American teams had won gold medals in 12 of 14 Olympiads, with an overall record of 117 victories and only two losses, dating back to 1936. Unfortunately, the 2004 group was assembled at the last minute, lost three times (more than in all previous Olympiads combined), and won only a bronze medal.

What had gone wrong? What was the missing ingredient? The players themselves were as talented as their predecessors. But instead of a team, it was simply a collection of individuals who hadn't been given the time to develop relationships, to connect to one another, and play together. It was a "team" in name only.

For USA Basketball officials, it was a hard-learned lesson, and a mistake they wouldn't repeat. The players for 2008 were chosen early and, given the opportunity to build the relationships so essential for team *work*, won all eight of their Olympic contests and the gold medal.

The last in the *Fortune* series (October 30, 2006) was titled "What It Takes to Be Great," profiling an all-star cast from the worlds of manufacturing, retailing, sports, entertainment, and high tech. In summarizing the magazine's findings, Geoffrey Colvin writes, "The good news is that your lack of a natural gift is irrelevant—talent has little or nothing to do with greatness . . . greatness isn't handed to anyone; it requires a lot of hard work."

Admittedly, this is a rather broad-brush overview of this "Secrets of Greatness" series in a major business magazine, but what I found most surprising was the complete lack of anything surprising. There were no great secrets revealed. These highly successful men and women do what successful people have always done.

Take out the references to email, BlackBerrys, laptops, cell phones, and other modern day conveniences, and there'd probably be little difference between these articles, written in 2006, and any secrets of success articles written hundreds—or even thousands—of years earlier.

What *was* surprising, however, was that among the many successful people profiled, greatness was something that was primarily inferred, rather than conferred. I found it difficult, however, to escape the conclusion—or at least the implication—that in achieving success one automatically dons the mantle of greatness.

Certainly, greatness can never be self-conferred, nor did any of the men and women profiled by *Fortune* even hint at it. To the contrary, as we'll soon see, many of their stories contain an underlying theme—a common ingredient—that enabled them to ascend the ladder of success and, perhaps, greatness.

A Different View

In his newest book, *Outliers: The Story of Success*, internationally best-selling author Malcolm Gladwell (*The Tipping Point* and *Blink*) echoes the importance of hard work in order to be successful. "The people at the very top don't work just harder or even much harder than everyone else," he writes. "They work much, *much* harder."

While the *Fortune* writers and Gladwell agree on the importance of hard work as a key to success, there are significant differences in their overall studies of what it takes to get there. For example, while the former series features numerous profiles of organizations and individuals in a wide range of activities, Gladwell takes a much different approach.

Gladwell, referring to *Outliers*, said, "The premise of this book is that you can learn a lot more about success by looking around at the successful person, at what culture they belong to, what their parents did for a living. Successful people are people who have made the most of a series of gifts that have been given to them by their culture or their history, by their generation."

For example, his research indicates that in some cases, the year—or even the month—a person was born is key. "The culture we belong to," he writes in *Outliers*, "and the legacies passed down by our forebears shape the patterns of our achievement in ways we cannot begin to imagine."

While Gladwell makes a convincing case for the importance of generation, family, culture, and class to become successful, his exhaustive research also led him to this conclusion: "No one—not rock stars, not professional athletes, not software billionaires, and not even geniuses—ever makes it alone."

An Underlying Thread

While there was no major focus on relationships in the *Fortune* series, a careful reading of the articles reveals a thread of connectedness, of relying on others, running through many of them. For example, the opening story, about Thomas Edison, begins with this statement: "He did his best work after dark." The story goes on to describe the inventor's all-night work sessions, quoting him as saying: "I owe my success to the fact that I never had a clock in my workroom."

But Edison didn't spend those long nights in isolated labor. According to this article, "the inventor would push himself and his dozen-plus researchers until dawn." Clearly not a lone ranger,

Edison once explained what it was that drove him: "I never perfected an invention that I did not think about in terms of the service it might give others. I find out what the world needs, then I proceed to invent."

Carlos Ghosn, CEO of both France's Renault and Japan's Nissan, spends much of his time flying to his offices, not just in three different countries—Japan, France, and the United States—but on three separate continents! Maintaining such a demanding schedule while handling enormous responsibilities would be all but impossible were it not for the bilingual assistants he has in each office. Yet Ghosn refuses to let his heavy work schedule disrupt his connectedness to his family. He told *Fortune,* "I do not bring my work home. I play with my four children and spend time with my family on weekends."

Amy W. Schulman, a partner in DLA Piper, a global law firm with offices all across the United States and in nearly two dozen other countries, told *Fortune,* "There isn't anybody on my team I don't trust 100%. Remember, I've been building this team for ten years."

James McNerney held top leadership positions at General Electric and then 3M before joining The Boeing Company, where he serves as chairman and CEO. Asked about his leadership philosophy, he told *Fortune,* "I start with people's growth . . . in terms of helping others get better."

A look behind the scenes at Boeing clearly demonstrates just how much emphasis the company places on people's growth, on building relationships, and developing the company's future leaders. One example is the Boeing Leadership Center (BLC), housed on a 286-acre campus near St. Louis. The stated goal of the BLC is "to allow leaders, from first-line managers to senior executives, to share what they're doing and what they're learning, as well as exchange techniques and best practices." A key part of the BLC is its Leaders Teaching Leaders (LTL) process, in which Boeing executives from all across the company share their expertise with participants in a format which encourages open discussion, questions and challenges. The program's ultimate goal is to build the company's leaders of tomorrow.

After her participation in the LTL program, one executive, Ginger Barnes, vice president, Weapons Programs, summed it up well. "Leadership," she said, "is all about leaders teaching leaders and about relationships."

There's that "R" word again—relationships! Regardless of the field—politics, sports, music, high tech, military, science, law, manufacturing, merchandising—the importance of relationships, of connectivity, is expressed again and again.

Where Greatness Lies

Once again, I pose the question I asked earlier: How do we define greatness? Surely, it can't be measured simply by how much money we have in the bank, by the size or success of the organizations we run, or by the size of our investment portfolios. And the awards and accolades we have displayed on our walls, no matter how many, don't proclaim our greatness.

Is success an accurate gauge of greatness? I don't think so. The pages of history are filled with the stories of men and women who enjoyed great success in their chosen fields of endeavor, yet for one reason or another never achieved greatness. Often, their success came at the expense of those they elbowed aside or climbed over, in their relentless efforts to reach the top rung of the ladder.

The Preacher and the Pitcher

Based on my experience—and on the hundreds of definitions and opinions I've gathered in my research on success—there's one ingredient that stands out in my mind as capturing its true meaning. Many of the men or women in articles and books on success make some reference to it, and Gladwell hit the nail on the head, but there are a couple of stories that illustrate it well. They're not about any business titans or captains of industry, but by a baseball player and a minister.

William Booth was an itinerant preacher walking the streets of London in 1865, bringing a message of hope to homeless men and women. From that modest beginning, the organization he founded, The Salvation Army, has now spread to more than 100 countries, and is generally acknowledged as perhaps the finest, best run, and most respected and successful organization of its kind in the world. And it was Booth who was able to distill this essential ingredient of greatness and success into a single word.

One Christmas, General Booth wished to send a Christmas greeting to his troops who, by then, were scattered in more than 50 countries around the world, encouraging them to continue serving the hurting and the needy. At that time, the only means of rapid communication was by telegram, which was expensive, with costs based on the number of words used. A practical and frugal man, General Booth found a single word to convey his message. His Christmas telegram read, simply: "Others."

The ballplayer's career ended more than 60 years ago, but what a career it was. A left-handed pitcher, who was later elected to the Baseball Hall of Fame, he helped the New York Yankees win seven American League championships and five World Series. He won more than 20 games in each of four seasons, was the winning pitcher in three All-Star games, and had a record of six wins and no losses in World Series games.

Yet, he never let his success get the better of him. A zany and colorful character, his antics and his sense of humor had earned him the nickname of "El Goofy." Once, when asked what had made him so successful, Vernon "Lefty" Gomez replied, "The secret of my success was clean living—and a fast outfield."

It was the kind of humorous comment for which he was famous, but perhaps without realizing it, he revealed a key ingredient in what distinguishes greatness from success: giving credit to others! Incidentally, during much of Gomez' outstanding career, the star of that "fast outfield" he gave credit to was the incomparable Joe DiMaggio.

Gomez' record is indisputable evidence of his success in his chosen field. But it was crediting others for that success that was a mark of his greatness. While success can be achieved without greatness, I'm convinced that everyone who earns the mantle of greatness has indeed reached the pinnacle of success.

Of course, one doesn't have to search the annals of business very deeply to uncover many examples of men and women who achieved greatness because of their concern for others.

A Business Philosophy Called PSP

It's a story that has taken on legendary proportions in the annals of business. It began with a term paper written in 1962 by a Yale freshman majoring in economics who had an idea for a new method and system for overnight package delivery. But it would be several more years before Frederick W. "Fred" Smith could act on that idea.

After graduating from Yale in 1966, Smith joined the Marine Corps, serving two tours in Vietnam, earning the Silver Star, Bronze Star, and two Purple Hearts. In 1969, he was honorably discharged with the rank of Captain. Two years later, he founded Federal Express (later changed to FedEx). The first few years were difficult ones, but the young company turned the corner in 1976, its first profitable year.

Today, FedEx operates in more than 200 countries, with a workforce of more than 290,000 employees and contractors and annual revenues approaching $40 billion. Asked in a 1998 interview with The Academy of Achievement for the primary reason for such phenomenal success, Smith explained: "First and foremost is our corporate philosophy, which we call PSP: People, Service, Profit. If you're going to run a high service organization, you have to get the commitment of the people working for that organization right at the start."

Smith credits his Marine Corps service for teaching him about leading people and building relationships with them. In that same interview, he said, "there we were, out in the countryside in Vietnam, living together, eating together and obviously going through all sorts of things. I think I came up with a very, very different perspective than most people that end up in senior management positions about what people who wear blue collars think about things and how they react to things, and what you should do to try to be fair."

It occurred to me that Fred Smith's brief but powerful PSP philosophy covers all the building blocks of sound business relationships, and could easily and accurately be translated into another acronym: ECS—Employees (People), Service (Customers), Shareholders (Profit).

Champion of the "Little People"

Amadeo was born in 1870 in San Jose, California, the son of Italian immigrants. He was only seven when his father died. After his mother remarried, he quit school at age 14 to join his stepfather in the produce business. Five years later, he had become a full partner and, at age 31, he sold his interest in the thriving business to his employees.

Then, the now wealthy young man was invited to serve on the board of directors of a local savings and loan company. Before long, however, he became frustrated by its unwillingness to extend credit to the small businessmen and merchants in the area, many of them hard-working immigrants and other "little people" that Amadeo had come to know and respect during his years in the produce business.

Determined to help them, he decided to open a bank of his own, one that would serve the needs of all the people. So it was that, in 1904, 34-year-old Amadeo, better known as A.P. Giannini, opened the Bank of Italy, with the initial capital of $150,000 coming largely from his stepfather and some friends who knew him as a man of unswerving integrity. Later, as the bank grew and prospered, its name was changed to Bank of America.

Two years later, the great San Francisco earthquake and fire left the city in ruins, and the majority of the city's bankers planned to keep their doors closed for six months, allowing them time to rebuild. But Giannini would have none of it. Almost immediately, on a waterfront wharf, he used a plank supported by two wooden barrels as a makeshift desk and was back in business, making loans with no more collateral than a handshake.

Giannini was a true visionary. Determined to have a "democratic bank" serving the needs of everyone, poor and wealthy, he was the first banker in the nation to establish a statewide branch banking system. Its mission was simply "Building California," and it fulfilled that mission with a passion. Over the years, it helped nearly every California community find markets for its bond issues, and it was a leading lender to the state's agricultural and wine industries and to the then fledgling movie industry.

Throughout his life, Giannini remained determined to stay in close touch with "the little people." He took very little salary and disdained wealth, believing it would adversely impact those relationships. "Money itch is a bad thing," he said. "I never had that problem."

While Bank of America, like other major financial institutions, has experienced more difficult times of late, such was not the case under A.P. Giannini's watch. At the time of his death in 1949, it was the nation's largest bank, built primarily because of one man who firmly believed in the primary importance of relationships, as expressed in his credo that "serving the needs of others is the only legitimate business in the world today."

A Tale of Two Airlines

It had been a long and tiring trip so, as I boarded my plane for the four-hour flight back home, I was glad that my frequent-flier status had resulted in an upgrade to the comfort of first-class seating. As I started down the aisle, I noticed a well-dressed and distinguished looking man seated in the front row. He had all the earmarks of a successful executive and, from the way the flight attendants were hovering over him, it was apparent that he must be "somebody."

Once we were airborne, the attendants again began paying far more attention to him than to any of the other passengers. When I commented to my seatmate about it, he told me the target of all that attention was the chairman and CEO of that airline, one of the nation's largest. Ah, I thought, it's no wonder the crew was falling all over him.

But what struck me most was this man's reaction—or rather lack thereof—to all this attention. There were few smiles and no small talk with any of the crew. In fact, not once during our four hours in the air did I even see him speak to any of the passengers unless they came up to speak to him. What a missed opportunity to build some goodwill with—and say thanks to—the very folks who were keeping his company flying, especially during the perilous times of upheaval and uncertainty his airline and the industry as a whole were experiencing.

One exception to that uncertainty was and is Southwest Airlines, which has continued to enjoy growth and success, while others have teetered on the brink of financial disaster. The primary reason, of course, has been the attitude modeled by its co-founder and former chairman and CEO, the legendary Herb Kelleher, and instilled in every company employee.

The notion of him sitting quietly on a Southwest flight while employees showered him with attention is absurd. Equally absurd would be trying to picture that other airline CEO appearing in public dressed as Elvis. That's something Kelleher often did, as a way of demonstrating that you can have fun without losing sight of your responsibilities, and that it's okay not to take yourself seriously as long as you do your job well.

Kelleher often walked the terminal in the airport and took Southwest flights just to visit with passengers and employees, getting their feedback on how well the company was doing its job and what it could do better. One of the major reasons for his success was his focus on people—on building relationships—not just on running an airline.

In an article in the newsletter of The McCombs School of Business Management at the University of Texas (Spring/Summer 2003) he told his interviewer, "We're in the customer service business and we happen to operate an airline. But then any business is about providing great customer service to the people you serve. We just happen to be in one branch of the customer service business."

"Customers are like a force of nature," he once wrote in an article for the Peter F. Drucker Foundation. "You can't fool them, and you ignore them at your own peril."

But on Kelleher's relationship ladder, one category ranks even higher than customers: his employees. Shareholders occupy a lower rung. In that same McCombs interview, he explained, "If you treat your employees right, they're happy and proud and participative with respect to what they're doing. They manifest that attitude to your customers and your customers come back. And what's business all about but having your customers come back, which makes the shareholders happy."

There are, of course, many other factors that have contributed to the success Southwest Airlines has enjoyed for so many years, not the least of which has been a willingness to take risks, to innovate, and to fly in the face of the conventional wisdom about how best to run an airline. Nevertheless, it has been its unswerving commitment to connecting—with its employees, its customers, and its shareholders—that has been the solid foundation on which this great company has been built.

Our Brother's—and Sister's—Keeper!

Greatness can never be achieved in a vacuum. Whatever success we achieve can best be measured by the impact we've made on others—touched them personally, brought them with us, and perhaps triggered in them the best they had to give.

At about the dawning of the 20th century, a young man named George Matthew Adams was making a name for himself as a successful advertising salesman in Chicago. Over the course of the next 60 years, he would gain fame as an author, publisher, and syndicated columnist.

Among the many quotations attributed to him was this one: "Are we our 'Brother's Keeper'? We certainly are! If we had no regard for others' feelings or fortune, we would grow cold and indifferent to life itself. Bound up with selfishness, we could not hope for the success that could easily be ours."

On another occasion, Adams wrote, "There is no such thing as a 'self-made' person. We are made up of thousands of others. Every one who has ever done a kind deed for us, or spoken one word of encouragement to us, has entered into the make-up of our character and of our thoughts, as well as our success."

The Other Side of the Coin

The start of the 20th century also marked the birth of Antoine de Saint-Exupéry in France. Like Adams, he would gain fame as an author, although his first love was flying, which eventually cost him his life when his plane was shot down during World War II.

During the late 1930s, while recuperating from a plane crash, he wrote *Wind, Sand and Stars*, a book about flying. In it is a vivid passage that describes what can happen to people who are the neglected others in the world around us.

Riding on a commuter bus and listening to the conversations of some of the homeward-bound "worn out clerks" sitting near him, Saint-Exupéry writes:

> I heard them talking to one another in murmurs and whispers. They talked about illness, money, shabby domestic cares. Their talk painted the walls of the dismal prison in which these men had locked themselves up. And suddenly, I had a vision of the face of destiny. Old bureaucrat, my comrade, it is not you who are to blame. No one ever helped you to escape. . . . Nobody grasped you by the shoulder while there was still time. Now the clay of which you were shaped has dried and hardened, and naught in you will ever awaken the sleeping musician, the poet, the astronomer that possibly inhabited you in the beginning.

What a sad and dreary picture. Imagine how different the lives of those men might have been had someone grasped them by the shoulder "while there was still time," before the clay of which they were shaped had dried and hardened. Simply showing them they mattered, that someone cared, might well have awakened them, allowing them to reach heights beyond their wildest dreams.

Humorist, writer and lecturer Samuel L. Clemens, who died in 1910, was perhaps the most popular American celebrity of his time. Better known as Mark Twain, he was the author of such classics as *The Adventures of Tom Sawyer, A Connecticut Yankee in King Arthur's Court,* and *The Adventures of Huckleberry Finn.* It was Twain who, in my opinion, best summed up the essence of greatness when he wrote, "Great people are those who make others feel that they, too, can become great."

The Fine Print

Despite the overwhelming evidence of the importance of building relationships to don the mantle of greatness, it's surprising what little emphasis is placed on it in the literature of business and leadership. As is the case with the *Fortune* series, and in numerous books and articles we've researched, one must search long and hard to find reference to the key role relationships invariably play along the journey to success and greatness. It may be mentioned in passing, or buried in the fine print, like the messages that appear briefly and in tiny print at the bottom of many TV commercials.

No, greatness isn't measured by our assets, by our achievements, by the size of our investment portfolio, or by the awards and accolades we've received. Instead, I'm convinced it can best be measured by the impact we've made on others, by the way we've connected with them, touched them personally, brought them along with us, and perhaps inspired their best contributions. In the words of the late U.S. Senate Chaplain Dick Halverson, "Greatness is always in terms of giving, not getting."

The pages of history are filled with the stories of men and women who enjoyed great success in their chosen fields of endeavor, yet for one reason or another, never achieved greatness.

Greatness can never be achieved in a vacuum. Whatever success we achieve can best be measured by the impact we've made on others—touched them personally, brought them with us, and perhaps triggered in them the best they had to give.

While success can be achieved without greatness, I'm convinced that everyone who earns the mantle of greatness has indeed reached the pinnacle of success.

In Other Words

Greatness lies, not in being strong, but in the right use of strength . . . He is the greatest whose strength carries up the most hearts by the attraction of his own.

William Cullen Bryant

If there is any great secret of success in life, it lies in the ability to put yourself in the other person's place and to see things from his point of view—as well as your own.

Henry Ford

Man is much like a hole: the more you take away from him the bigger he gets. Greatness is always in terms of giving, not getting.

Richard C. Halverson

Communication—the human connection—is the key to personal and career success.

Paul J. Meyer

A great attitude does much more than turn on the lights in our worlds; it seems to magically connect us to all sorts of serendipitous opportunities that were somehow absent before we changed.

Earl Nightingale

The art of dealing with people is the foremost secret of successful men. A man's success in handling people is the very yardstick by which the outcome of his whole life's work is measured.

Paul C. Packer

The most important single ingredient in the formula of success is knowing how to get along with people.

Theodore Roosevelt

Nothing liberates our greatness like the desire to help, the desire to serve.

Marianne Williamson

CHAPTER 2

You Can Be a Connector Even If You're Not a Natural People Person

How Social Intelligence Makes a Major Difference in Business

Y ou might not *be* the type of person who loves to socialize, attend big parties, and network whenever you get the chance. If so, that's okay! This book is still for you. The key to being able to utilize relationships with your clients does not mean that you must create relationships with *everyone* who crosses your path. It simply requires you to have a plan for those with whom you would like to connect with; if you look at the future of your career and/or business, you'll immediately be able to identify people with whom it is important that you become well acquainted. First and foremost will be the customers that you want to turn into loyal clients for life. The more you understand what priority links you need to make, the sooner you will be able to take advantage of some of the common sense—and sometimes, even simple—principles of connecting. It doesn't matter whether you are introverted or extroverted; what matters is that you've spent some time thinking about which relationships are most vital and why.

Recently, probably the nation's best-known networking professional came to the realization that he is an introvert! Ivan Misner, PhD, founder of BNI and the author of 11 books on networking, shared with me that he recently discovered that he is actually an introvert. *What?* Misner said that his wife of 20 years told him during dinner one night that he displayed many introvert tendencies. Misner was shocked! How could a professional speaker and the founder of the largest networking organization be an introvert? So he took an online test and found that he was a "situational extrovert," meaning that he was reserved around strangers but very outgoing in the right context. "It struck me why I started BNI," Misner said. "I was naturally uncomfortable meeting new people. BNI created a system that enabled me to meet people in an organized, structured, networking environment that did not require that I actually . . . talk to strangers."

So, if we all can potentially be great networkers with other people, how do we jump into it or how can we focus to improve our skills and results?

The Connector Plan: Where Do I Start?

To begin forming potential connections, it's a good idea to first begin by figuring out with which people your most important relationships already and potentially exist. Ask yourself this: Who do I need to be able to connect with in order to create loyal clients, further my career, and build my business successes? (Hint: consider categories like clients and vendors or specific individuals within categories). Now list these ideas below:

Downloadable Form 2.1: CONNECTION LIST

1. _____
2. _____
3. _____
4. _____
5. _____
6. _____
7. _____
8. _____
9. _____
10. _____
11. _____
12. _____
13. _____
14. _____
15. _____
16. _____
17. _____
18. _____
19. _____
20. _____

*Go to *www.redzonemarketing.com/TheConnectors* to view an electronic form called "Connection List" for tracking contacts. Enter keycode "CONNECT" to download it for free!

Now, jot down some ideas for reaching out to each of these people, and set a due date to connect! We will discuss specific connection strategies as you move through this book.

Your Intelligence Is Important

Relationships in business are dynamic; thus, no one really is perfect at the skills that connecting requires. I, and many others, struggle to get better at it every day. And of course, there are some who are better than others at creating and cultivating relationships in business. However, you certainly don't have to be a born charismatic to win clients for life. For years I've been watching, researching, listening, observing, and recording the unique characteristics and traits that make up a connector.

The first thing that is important to recognize is that any good connector has a high level of intelligence, and I'm not talking about IQ-assessed intelligence. I'm talking about *social* intelligence, a type that's not measured with a broad brush like an IQ test. The "Most Likely to Succeed" (a frequently designated high school award) often does not identify the person who actually *does* succeed. Members of the high IQ group MENSA are also not all the most successful in business. But wait! If being the smartest person in the room does not equate to business success, then what does? I'd like to work to break the career-stopping myth that you need to be academically smart to succeed; it simply isn't true. There is a lot more to success. And it involves connecting with others!

Breaking the Myth of the IQ Test as a Success Measure

When Alfred Binet developed a measure to predict which students in Paris would succeed and which would fail in the primary grades at the beginning of the twentieth century, he started what was to become the intelligence quotient IQ assessment. The IQ test was then used with more than one million American military recruits for World War I. Since then the IQ subculture has expanded into the Scholastic Aptitude Test (SAT), the American College Test (ACT), the Graduate Record Examination (GRE), the Miller Analogies Test (MAT), and many others. *But none of them accurately predict success in business.* In fact, recent research has shown that IQ influences at best 25 percent of people's success in their career. Other analysis shows that actually IQ may account for no more than 4 percent to 10 percent of success.[1] Columbia University psychologist Edward L. Thorndike maintained that there are three main "intelligences": abstract, mechanical, and social. In a 1930s

Harper's Magazine article, Thorndike defined social intelligence as the ability to understand others and "act wisely in human relations." He maintained that social intelligence is different from academic ability, and that it's a key element in what makes people succeed in life.

Author Karl Albrecht defines social intelligence in his book, *Social Intelligence: The New Science of Success,*[2] as a combination of awareness of the feelings, needs, and interests of others—sometimes called your "social radar"—plus an attitude of generosity and consideration, and a set of practical skills for interacting successfully in various situations. Social Intelligence is one of at least six distinct intelligences or dimensions of human performance now recognized by scientists and educators. It should come as no surprise, therefore, that this particular aptitude plays such an important role in determining personal and professional success.

If You're So Smart, Why Aren't You Rich?

IQ measures long have been used to make distinctions between people; those with higher IQs are, of course, supposed to be superior to those with lower IQs. However, the identification of intelligence with financial success is the phenomenon that popularized the phrase, "If you're so smart, why aren't you rich?" After all, IQ tests merely tap an individual's capacity to:

1. Follow directions
2. Follow the right steps and arrive at the correct solution as defined by the person who developed the test
3. Memorize history, scientific data, and other facts and concepts

The difficulty with IQ-related definitions of intelligence is that they refer to certain qualities or skills that may lead to effectiveness or limited success; yet they do not account for the specific grouping of qualities we include in social intelligence. Yes, it takes a great mental skill to score high on an IQ test. *But it requires a great deal of psychological smarts to acquire wealth!*

If You're So Smart, Why Aren't You Doing Smart Things?

Theodore Kaczynski has been defined as a genius. He was a Harvard-educated Berkeley professor. But this genius turned into someone we came to know as the "Unabomber," who spent the years from 1978 through 1995 sending out mail bombs to various victims. How could someone so smart—with such a high IQ, an education from one of the world's best learning institutions, a professor—do something like this?

Kaczynski serves as a reminder that perhaps there is something fundamentally wrong with our identification of academic or logical-mathematical skill as "intelligence." After all, he was clearly someone who could not separate right from wrong or simply didn't care. If the concepts of intelligence were broadened to include social compassion and concern, then the Unabomber would not be considered at all intelligent.

We Are Sophisticated Beings and We Were Born to Connect

It is easy to recognize a special capacity that people have—some more so than others—to connect with others in a deep and direct way. We see this quality expressed by a performer in front of a screaming crowd, a teacher who has full control of her class, a leader who is loved by his or her subordinates, or a manager who is revered. To accomplish this, connectors essentially are sensing and stimulating the reactions and mood of others. That's what the connection is all about!

In 1995, Harvard University trained psychologist and *New York Times* writer Daniel Goleman published a book entitled *Emotional Intelligence*, in which he discussed the human ability "to manage our own emotions and inner potential for positive relationships."

Essentially, he claimed that our emotions play a much greater role in thought, decision making, and individual success than is commonly acknowledged. In his second book, *Social Intelligence: The New Science of Human Relationships*, Goleman increased the scope to include human abilities to connect with one another. "We are wired to connect," Goleman says. "Neuroscience has discovered that our brain's very design makes it sociable, inexorably drawn into an intimate brain-to-brain linkup whenever we engage with another person. That neural bridge lets us affect the brain—and so the body—of everyone we interact with, just as they do us."

Every interaction between people incites emotions and stimulates our nervous systems, hormones, heart rate, circulation, breathing, and the entire immune system. Goleman explains how given our socially reactive brains, we must "be wise," he says, and be aware of the ways that our moods influence the biology of each life we touch.[3]

Social Intelligence is the interpersonal part of emotional intelligence. If our brains are designed to connect with the brains of others, then our interactions are all a two-way street—causing action and reaction in every contact. It is kind of like a chattering between minds. It's what allows rapport and love and the basis of any effective interaction. Other people make us feel better or worse. But they *always* make us feel.

Does Social Intelligence Translate into Business Success?

Applying the theories of social intelligence has been proven to lead to better relationships with customers, faster closes, and less effort in the sales process. And customers will most likely increase their levels of support and respect for you. But it goes much deeper than that. People who have higher levels of social intelligence and connection abilities are also the great leaders. And, great leaders can do one very significant thing: They get people to act.

In 1998, Goleman published an article entitled "What Makes a Leader?" in the *Harvard Business Review*. People started to buzz about the role that bonding and relationships play in effective business and leadership. In fact, what was discovered is that certain things leaders do—specifically, exhibit empathy and become attuned to others' moods—literally affect both their own and their followers' brain chemistry. So we can draw the conclusion that a powerful way of becoming a better leader is to learn the kinds of social behavior that reinforce the brain's social circuitry. Goleman says, "Leading effectively is, in other words, less about mastering situations—or even social skill sets—than about developing a genuine interest in and talent for fostering positive feelings in the people whose cooperation and support you need."

The idea that leaders need social skills is not a new one, of course. In 1920, Thorndike pointed out that "the best mechanic in a factory may fail as a foreman for lack of social intelligence." Harvard's Claudio Fernández-Aráoz also found in an analysis of new C-level executives that those who had been hired for their self-discipline, drive, and intellect were sometimes later fired for lacking basic social skills. In other words, the people Fernández-Aráoz studied were incredibly intelligent, but their inability to get along socially on the job was detrimental to their success.

Applying social intelligence has been proven to lead to better relationships with customers, faster sales closes, and less effort in the sales process. And customers will most likely increase their levels of support and respect for you when social skills are at a higher level. But their abilities go much deeper than that. Socially intelligent people get people to act. This translates into people buying, moving, buzzing about, and following.

Social Intelligence and the Impact in Politics

Not surprisingly, the use of social intelligence skills is one of the key contributors to success in the political arena. Since the goal here is to garner a majority of people's support and votes in a particular area, the ability to connect with individuals is the most pronounced element in a successful political career. Consider the personal power of Ronald Reagan, Bill Clinton, and most recently,

Barack Obama and how they all attracted others to them as their most powerful characteristic.

Back in 1988, my first job out of college was to work in Wisconsin on the political campaign of Herb Kohl, who was running for United States Senate. Kohl was a multimillionaire former grocery store owner who had shifted his focus to political aspirations. He pronounced that he wanted to give back to the people of Wisconsin by becoming their representative in the Senate.

In his campaign, Kohl spent his own money to finance a majority of the campaign; some had credited that for his initial election success. But if one looked back at his successes in business and his first political win and how both happened, there was much more in play than simply deep pockets.

As I was working on the campaign, I realized firsthand that Kohl connected with people on a different level than most others did. Herb Kohl looks like an average person; he doesn't dress in the most expensive clothes or drive fancy cars. But when he meets someone, he makes an undeniable and memorable impression. He shakes your hand for longer than usual as he looks at your face and appears to be memorizing it—and he is. He listens carefully to the person who is speaking to him with incredible focus and intensity. There is no doubt that after speaking to Kohl, you feel differently about him because of the way his actions show that he truly cares. It is unusual. And, he does it in the same way with the same success to this day.

When I needed to recruit volunteer campaign workers to help organize rallies, put up campaign signs, and get out the vote, the first place we always looked was at Kohl's former employees. These former employees who had worked for Kohl at his family-owned grocery store chain, Kohl's Food Stores, were his most loyal supporters. They were the first to help when I called and the ones who seemed the most passionate about his hopeful success in politics. They absolutely loved him!

I asked some of these former employees why they felt the way they did about Herb Kohl. They would tell me, "Oh, Herb knows me, he knows everyone who worked for him." And Kohl truly *did* know their names and the names of their children. He asked questions when he saw them, and he never forgot a face, a name, or a story. Because of his inherent capacity to connect with others, our most loyal campaign workers were the army of grocery store workers who didn't just work for him in the past, but truly felt like they had a relationship with him. There were hundreds and hundreds of them throughout the state! Kohl won the election in a landslide because of his ability to use his high social intelligence to connect with people in a sustaining manner. It wasn't Kohl's money that built relationships; it was his knack for understanding and getting along with others.

Senator Kohl is still a sitting senator today. He is one of the very most popular individuals in the state of Wisconsin by opinion polls. He is a philanthropist, the owner of the state's NBA basketball team, the Milwaukee Bucks, and a public servant for more than 20 years. He is a giver and a connector. And his success and popularity come from the way he makes people feel.

What Is It about Being Socially Intelligent That Gets People to Act, Buy, and Follow?

It is quite simple. It's how you make them feel.

A significant discovery in behavioral neuroscience is the identification of *mirror neurons* in widely dispersed areas of the brain. Italian neuroscientists found these by accident while monitoring a particular cell in a monkey's brain that fired only when the monkey raised its arm. One day, a lab assistant lifted an ice cream cone to his own mouth and triggered a reaction in the monkey's cell. It was the first evidence that the brain is peppered with neurons that mimic, or mirror, what another being does. This previously unknown class of brain cells operates as neural Wi-Fi, allowing us to navigate our social world. When we consciously or unconsciously detect someone else's emotions through their actions, our mirror neurons reproduce those emotions. Collectively, these neurons create an instant sense of shared experience, and that causes a feeling which proceeds the actions.[4]

Is Social Intelligence a Learnable Skill?

While some people seem to be more naturally sociable than others, social intelligence *is* something that can be taught and learned. We can improve and translate our social intelligence into becoming a better connector in our business relationships, and ultimately find dramatically more success. You simply have to pinpoint the areas you need to work on and how to go about doing this.

I often use assessments with my clients, which I've personally found to be incredibly insightful, to assist them in increasing their self-awareness, social intelligence, and ability to connect. There are many tools available to gauge our personality and interpersonal skills. We typically use our Connector IQ (C-IQ) Assessment, which is available for you to take in the next Chapter of this book. This test essentially scores your connector proficiency and, more importantly, brings awareness to your strengths and weaknesses in connecting.

Another assessment broadly used by businesses—and one that I've become certified to administer—is called the Fundamental Interpersonal Relations Orientation (FIRO-B). This assessment tool provides information about some fundamental interpersonal dimensions in these areas:

- *Inclusion:* How much you include other people in your life, and how much attention, contact, and recognition you want from others.

- *Control:* How much influence and responsibility you express, and how much you want others to lead and influence you.

- *Affection:* How close and warm you are with others, and how close and warm you want others to be with you.

The Center for Creative Leadership in Greensboro, North Carolina, conducted a study that discovered that only one of the three FIRO-B dimensions differentiated the top quartile of business leaders from the bottom quartile, and it may not be what you think it is.

While it's often assumed that successful businesspeople exhibited control in order to be the most effective, that is not what the research has found. The single factor that differentiated top business leaders from those at the bottom was affection—how much a leader expresses it, as well as how much he or she desires it. In other words, the highest performing leaders show—and want to receive—more warmth than the bottom 25 percent. The leaders who are most effective are those who are able to make connections, engage, and encourage others. They take what they hear from followers into account to make the best decisions. How might you increase your own ability to connect, engage, and encourage?

Now you will have a chance to assess exactly where you are in terms of your social intelligence development. In the next chapter, our C-IQ Assessment will help you focus on your own current state of connecting.

CHAPTER 3

The Connector IQ
Assessment

Am I Socially Intelligent?

W e are living in an era during which the ability to create effective business relationships and connect with others is becoming more important than ever for success. A businessperson's ability to establish meaningful relationships is in fact essential, as our world becomes more connected technologically, but less so physically. Those who are able to create bonds, engage others, and develop impactful business relationships have—and will—open doors that create a visible path to success.

How might you increase your own ability to connect? To determine what type of a connector you are, take the following assessment. It is designed to increase your awareness only as to the kind of connector you may be.

The Connector IQ (C-IQ) Assessment

Answer these questions as they apply to you RIGHT NOW (not what you would like the answers to be). Be honest, as this assessment is designed only for your use and awareness.

1. I look for opportunities to connect with other professionals.

Daily	Weekly	Monthly	Yearly	Never
(4)	(3)	(2)	(1)	(0)

2. I look for ways to connect people I know with each other.

Daily	Weekly	Monthly	Yearly	Never
(4)	(3)	(2)	(1)	(0)

3. I am interested and ask about the businesses of others.

Always	Often	Sometimes	Infrequently	Never
(4)	(3)	(2)	(1)	(0)

4. I reach out to people in my network proactively.

Daily	Weekly	Monthly	Yearly	Never
(4)	(3)	(2)	(1)	(0)

5. I ask a lot of questions of others.

Always	Often	Sometimes	Infrequently	Never
(4)	(3)	(2)	(1)	(0)

6. I listen more than talk in conversations.

Always	Often	Sometimes	Infrequently	Never
(4)	(3)	(2)	(1)	(0)

7. I look for ways to refer people I know to others.

Daily	Weekly	Monthly	Yearly	Never
(4)	(3)	(2)	(1)	(0)

8. I reach out to a mentor.

Daily	Weekly	Monthly	Yearly	Never
(4)	(3)	(2)	(1)	(0)

9. I am actively involved in professional organizations.

Daily	Weekly	Monthly	Yearly	Never
(4)	(3)	(2)	(1)	(0)

10. I systematically keep in touch with other professionals.

Daily	Weekly	Monthly	Yearly	Never
(4)	(3)	(2)	(1)	(0)

11. I use social media.

Daily	Weekly	Monthly	Yearly	Never
(4)	(3)	(2)	(1)	(0)

12. I collaborate with my employees/colleagues and get consensus decisions on new ideas.

Always	Often	Sometimes	Infrequently	Never
(4)	(3)	(2)	(1)	(0)

13. I try to make interactions with me memorable for others.

Always	Often	Sometimes	Infrequently	Never
(4)	(3)	(2)	(1)	(0)

14. I focus on making conversations, presentations and meetings ALL about the other people and what is important to them.

Always	Often	Sometimes	Infrequently	Never
(4)	(3)	(2)	(1)	(0)

15. I send personal notes or individual personal emails to others.

Daily	Weekly	Monthly	Yearly	Never
(4)	(3)	(2)	(1)	(0)

16. I use active listening techniques.

Always	Often	Sometimes	Infrequently	Never
(4)	(3)	(2)	(1)	(0)

17. I engage in personal conversations with business associates.

Always	Often	Sometimes	Infrequently	Never
(4)	(3)	(2)	(1)	(0)

18. I disclose personal information about myself with business contacts.

Always	Often	Sometimes	Infrequently	Never
(4)	(3)	(2)	(1)	(0)

19. I invite participation of others when making business decisions.

Always	Often	Sometimes	Infrequently	Never
(4)	(3)	(2)	(1)	(0)

20. I plan for expanding my network of professionals.

Daily	Weekly	Monthly	Yearly	Never
(4)	(3)	(2)	(1)	(0)

Add up the number under your selection for each of the 20 questions. Relate your totals to the following.

Connector IQ Types

Score of 60–80 = POWER CONNECTOR

You reach out mostly daily to others, engage, and proactively create and maintain relationships. You have established a focus on interaction with others; you most likely have empathy for, are genuinely curious about, and feel a compelling need to connect with other people. You are a Power Connector.

Score of 40–59 = ENERGY CONNECTOR

You reach out to others, but probably not on a daily basis. You may find that others reach out to connect with you as frequently as or more than you reach out to them. You have a great interest in others, and you want to connect and engage. You know relationships in your business are important, but you don't focus on this importance every day. You are an Energy Connector.

Score of 39 or below = CASUAL CONNECTOR

You reach out to others, but not as a focus in your business. You most likely create strong relationships with others but do not want to or do not have an interest in increasing relationships with large numbers of people. You connect with others more reactively than proactively. You are a Casual Connector.

So now that you have your Connector Factor, let's take this information and a willingness to improve—even just a little—and turn it into the kind of success of some of the world's most successful businesspeople.

Improving Your Connector IQ: Awareness Is the First Step

The most important first action is simply awareness. Once you know something about yourself, you can begin to improve. Think about this: If you became aware that you had been unintentionally doing something that was negative to others around you that you cared about, you would most likely make a change, right?

In business, we look at our marketing strategies and sales tactics when trying to reach our business goals. In fact, these are the same places that we look when we are *not* reaching our goals. Sometimes our lack of growth may be due to something else entirely; however, we don't know this until we can assess our situation.

One of the entrepreneurs with whom we work at Red Zone Marketing has always had an incredible desire to get to the next level in her business, but for awhile, she wasn't experiencing very significant results. She had made a commitment to marketing and business development; read every book and publication she could get her hands on; had numerous, high-level industry certifications; and attempted to hire the best and the brightest employees. Yet she still had not achieved the level of success she desired. Referrals kept going down year after year. Additional business from current clients was stagnant. And new client acquisition seemed to be getting more and more difficult.

After much investigation into her operations and several interviews with her clients and staff, the challenge to our client's growth was uncovered: We discovered that her employees were at the center of the problem. Unfortunately, her staff did not have the same passion that she did for helping this business succeed and did not respect her decision making. Furthermore, the personal interviews and surveys that we conducted allowed us to identify the reason for this: It was because of the way our client continually made her employees feel. She was a very hard worker herself, very demanding of others, and wanted the best for her clients above all else. But, in essence, we discovered that her people simply didn't like her.

When we shared the findings with this entrepreneur (a tough message to hear and to deliver), she was shocked! Her face went white. She was simply not aware of her demeanor toward her staff, nor did she have any inkling about how they felt toward her. Her goal to succeed was actually being taken down by . . . herself? "As if we don't have enough challenges in business," she said. "And my biggest problem is me?"

Our client clearly cared about her staff, but in her drive to succeed and serve clients, she had lost sight of the main ingredient of a successful business. Her staff had a majority of the day-to-day contact with clients, and their lack of passion and commitment to service was transparent. They weren't working in the best interest of the firm, because they were not committed to the company for the long term.

Once this business owner realized the impact she was having on her staff, she altered her behavior immediately—*literally*. As soon as she heard the findings, she called an impromptu staff meeting. She told the employees how she felt about them. She shared a story about her fear of failure, having watched her grandfather fail in business, and how painful that was for her family. She shared that her professional goal had always been to help enough people so she'd never fail. She gave them some background on why she was who she was. She finished by saying one nice personal thing about each and every person in the meeting. Needless to say, her staff realized that something was changing, but frankly, they didn't believe it would last.

However, this entrepreneur's solution was something totally within her control. Her solution was to focus on herself, her actions, and her reactions. She never tried to deflect blame or get upset at her staff. After much consideration about changes in the firm, she determined that in the future, she wouldn't give her staff more time off (they already received 3-plus weeks vacation), and she didn't plan an all-staff retreat to a plush place. She simply respected them differently than she did before—in every interaction—because she was now aware.

Make no mistake, this type of change did not take place easily or magically happen overnight. At the end of every day, she reviewed and gave a few minutes of introspection to the following items:

1. Review the day and the interactions with staff and clients.

2. Rate today's positive impact on others (Grade A-F).
3. Write down the notable successes and failures from the day.

The more time she spent reviewing these interactions, the better she became at recognizing the effect her actions and words potentially had on her staff. She began to anticipate how people might react to things she may say; she rehearsed conversations in advance; and she developed a vision for herself and for her change. Such mental preparation strengthens the neural connections in the brain that are needed to act effectively; in fact, this is the reason that athletes, dancers, actors, pilots, and other precision professionals put hundreds of hours into mental review of their moves also.

The results of the changes she made were obvious in her business. All of the firm's objectives began moving in a different direction. Referrals from current clients doubled over a one-year period. Business increased year over year 23 percent, and it is now a completely different place to walk into. She found the success for which she had been searching for so long—simply because she became aware of how she related to other people.

Are *you* aware of how you connect with others?

Other Helpful Assessments Available

The following are several more possibilities for assessing your own connectability with others.

FIRO-B: *Fundamental Interpersonal Relations Orientation*

FIRO is a theory of interpersonal relations introduced by renowned psychologist William Schutz in 1958. According to Schutz's theory, three dimensions of interpersonal relations are necessary and sufficient to explain most human interaction: inclusion, control, and affection. These categories measure how much interaction a person wants in the areas of socializing, leadership, and responsibilities.

FIRO-B, a measurement instrument with scales that assess the behavioral aspects of the three dimensions, was created based on this theory. Scores are graded from 0–9 in scales of expressed and wanted behavior, which define how much a person expresses to others and how much he wants from others. From this, Schutz identified the following types:

Inclusion:
1. Undersocial
2. Oversocial
3. Social

Control types
1. Abdicrat
2. Autocrat
3. Democrat

Affection types
1. Underpersonal
2. Overpersonal
3. Personal

Myers-Briggs Type Indicator (MBTI)

MBTI is a widely used personality inventory or test that is often employed in business and education to evaluate personality type in adolescents and adults age 14 and older. Millions of people take the MBTI each year, making it the most frequently used personality inventory available. The test was first introduced in 1942 as the work of mother and daughter Katharine C. Myers Briggs and Isabel Briggs. There are now several different versions of the test available, but form M, which contains 93 items, is the most commonly used.

The Myers-Briggs inventory is based on Carl Jung's theory of types, outlined in his 1921 work *Psychological Types*. Jung's theory holds that human beings are either *introverts* or *extraverts*, and their behavior follows from these inborn psychological types. He also believed that people take in and process information different ways, based on their personality traits.

The Myers-Briggs evaluates personality type and preference based on the four Jungian psychological types:

- extraversion (E) or introversion (I)
- sensing (S) or intuition (N)
- thinking (T) or feeling (F)
- judging (J) or perceiving (P)

The Kolbe Index

The Kolbe A Index measures a person's instinctive method of operation (MO) and identifies the ways he or she will be most productive. It is assessing innate action modes that, according to Kolbe, do not change over time. To give an example: People with different profiles might respond to a challenge differently. Let's say that the particular challenge is to learn Swedish. You may do it based on the four modes of action that individuals possess:

- *Quick Start:* If you're a Quick Start who wants to learn Swedish, you'll probably buy a learning system online and begin to practice by calling a few friends and speaking in broken Swedish until you get good at it. You will jump right into trial and error.
- *Fact Finder:* You'll spend hours reading about, researching, asking questions, and learning about the nuances of the Swedish language before actually beginning to start learning it.
- *Implementor:* You will sit in on a course being given at the local college.
- *Follow Through:* You'll likely register for the course at the local college and read the books they give each night as the lesson plan dictates.

Understanding the Personality and Style of Others

Understanding your clients' and prospects' personalities will help you become better prepared for managing their expectations—an important factor in client satisfaction and client loyalty. The financial advisors with whom we have worked—and professionals in most industries—agree that understanding people is nearly as important as understanding the core product, in this case, investments. The ability to quickly assess a client's personality and needs is a foremost skill of a successful investment advisor and will have dramatic effects in getting the client to take action quicker and developing the desired long-term, loyal client.

For instance, an advisor's conversation with an investor may be centered on the big picture of the entire portfolio and avoid the details of the individual, underlying investments. That is how the advisor would like to hear the information—"Just tell me where I'm at." But that client may be much more intently focused on the details of the individual investments, their history, and why they are in the portfolio, rather than looking at the big picture of the entire portfolio only. The connection will not be established if there is a division between the communication and information delivered.

It's important in connecting to understand yourself and others, and then be able to assimilate yourself to the type of person with whom you are connecting. Even more so, according to Daniel Goleman in *Social Intelligence*, "it is about synchronizing movements and mannerisms during interaction. The more the movements are matched, the more positive the feelings about the interaction."

What motivates your clients and prospects to act? The reasons people make decisions tend to be deeply personal. All clients are not created equal. It's extremely helpful to understand the personality of the person with whom you are communicating—whether you're taking part in a conversation or delivering a sales presentation. Personality has a major impact on buying behavior; if you can craft your communications to fit your clients' personality type, you'll be more able to effectively get others to act. And when you're keenly aware of your *own* personality type, you can better identify with your clients and know how they differ from you—so as not to use your own preferences in your presentation to them.

Author Mitch Anthony states in his book *Selling with Emotional Intelligence* that when clients have a choice they are most likely to go with the option that presents the least amount of emotional annoyance. If you are able to pinpoint the client personality type, it will become easier for you to understand how they may intake information, their propensity for certain action, and how they may be likely to feel about decisions and outcomes.

CHAPTER 4

The Red Zone Connectors Formula

The Principles for Building Valuable Relationships

When you assessed your Connector IQ, were you at all surprised? I think the least surprising thing about taking this assessment is that there is almost always room for improvement. If you are a great connector and have used your skills to build relationships with clients and increase business or you are someone who doesn't yet have a high level of confidence in your connection abilities, you can always get better—even if it's just a little bit.

At Red Zone Marketing, we look at the ability to improve—even sometimes just tweak—what *is* working as a great, and sometimes overlooked, opportunity. To use a football analogy, you are in the red zone (within 20 yards of the goal line). You are within scoring distance, and you have the ability to make a touchdown. But the amount of time that it takes you get to the end zone to score—and get back there to do it again—can be the difference be-tween average and extraordinary levels of success. If you want to get to the next level, have a better year than last, and have the success you desire, the key is often to find a way to close more sales. You want to be able to close bigger sales, with less effort, and more quickly. If you want to have more loyal client relationships, you first need to gather more clients.

So how do the best connectors do both—acquire new business and *cultivate lasting relationships with the clients they have acquired?* Instead of merely telling you *what* they do, our goal is to share *how* they do it. We believe it is a given that relationships in business are impor-tant. The purpose is to describe in more detail the specific skills and traits that are being used by successful businesspeople to actually form better relationships.

Connecting More Effectively Using The 5 Red Zone Connector Traits

In addition to considering our clients at Red Zone Marketing, we have researched and interviewed some of the most notable busi-nesspeople and connectors—those who have made a living out of creating relationships in business. Our research and observations have clearly defined five areas or traits that most of these excep-tional people possess. They are the traits that have guided and pre-cipitated their ability to connect with others and create extraordinary sales. They are simple and common sense, but they are qualities that most others do not carry out with consistency and/or proficiency.

These successful individuals use their intelligence—their social intelligence—and put it to work every day in their quest to forward their business goals, increase sales, and create lasting client relationships.

In the next section of this book, we will go over each of these in detail. The following is a summary of the Red Zone Connector Traits:

1. Develop a True "What's in It for Them" Mentality: *Focusing on Others Brings More for You*
   Maintaining focus on other people is not nearly as simple as it may sound. After all, we are hardwired to concentrate heavily on ourselves; it is our natural instinct. But, when we are more outward focused and truly connected to the others around us—how they feel, how things affect them, why they should care—it literally changes everything.
   When clients and employees are treated with the same respect as your closest friends, that focus can be equated to how much you care about them. And, it causes them to feel differently about you because of the way you respect them. So in making it about them you also make it about you.
   Great sales people and leaders who have been able to focus on others have found success in creating the type of relationships that truly win clients for life. But the most amazing thing is that these relationships can be created even if they don't really know each other.
   Example of a "What's in It for Them" person: Oprah Winfrey. Oprah's entire career has been about other people, helping them and giving them self-improvement ideas, book recommendations, and entertainment. Oprah is someone who truly has others in mind and is the ultimate example of a giver. She is one of the wealthiest people in the world and has a loyal following that watch and read her words nearly every day.

2. Listen—*Curiously* Listen: *Connecting is Not about Being A Great Talker*
   Are you good at listening? That's a pretty interesting question; because listening, which is vastly different from merely hearing, is an acquired skill. *Active* listening requires that the listener receive both the speaker's spoken and unspoken message. This can be difficult because very often the listener is so busy thinking about responding to what the speaker is saying that he misses much of what the speaker is trying to convey. Listening exceptionally is important to understanding what the speaker is saying. But almost as important is the

perception that others will have of you if you are a completely focused empathetic and active listener.

Example of a Curious Listener: Lee Iacocca. Iacocca credits his success as a leader and a former CEO with Chrysler with his ability to be a good listener. "A leader has to show curiosity. He has to listen to people outside of the 'Yes, sir' crowd in his inner circle. Businesspeople need to listen at least as much as they need to talk. Too many people fail to realize that real communication goes in both directions."

3. Important Questions to Ask That Attract Connections: *Getting Others to Do the Work!*
It's hard to listen if the other member of your exchange isn't doing much talking. To really connect with someone, you need to ask good questions that show you are interested, help you learn, and will allow you to use your listening skills.
Example of Someone Who Used Questions to Learn and Listen: Jack Welch. ("Neutron Jack?" A Connector? Yes!) Although Jack Welch is thought of as a great business leader, he's not necessarily known for his softer, relationship side. But his relationship skills actually played a key role in building GE. To Welch, the legendary former CEO of General Electric, business leadership was all about connecting with his employees and knowing what questions to ask them and when. To understand the strategic issues within each of GE's businesses and to see where these business units were going, Welch perfected the act of asking good questions. From there he received the information he needed to make smart decisions and help lead his team.

4. Get the Sale to Close Itself: *Using Creative Strategies to Sell without Pushing What You Have*
A relationship can be broken when traditional sales tactics are used. We have found that great connectors are able to close more sales and make it look easier in the process by utilizing and leveraging the work they've put into their relationships. In fact, they rarely have to sell. The sale closes itself because there is an overwhelming desire on the part of the buyer to buy. If someone wants what you have, wants to follow, wants to act, the sale just closes itself. Great leaders are

always closing, but mostly you don't know it. Their passion is so strong you find yourself along on their ride.

Example of Someone Who Used Skills to Get the Sale to Close Itself: Fred Smith is the visionary entrepreneur who founded Federal Express. Smith was called a business evangelist. His employees worked for no pay during difficult times because his conviction and belief in overnight package delivery stayed strong. Smith conveyed great power and emotion to his employees while giving them a reason to believe and a path to follow. He used his passion for the business to create loyal employees first and then a following of loyal clients next. You don't need to close sales using hard selling tactics when people want to do business with you; passion sells!

5. Create a Memorable Experience: *Differentiating Yourself by the Impact You Leave on Others*

   The definition of an "experience" is delivering the unexpected, something that makes you say, "Wow!" The norm is what is *expected*; the surprisingly positive is what creates the experience and is what makes people feel differently. And, it is the experience that creates an attraction that keeps them coming back.

   Example of Someone who Created an Experience: Dave Thomas was the founder of Wendy's Old Fashioned Hamburger restaurants, and he appeared as himself in the hamburger company's advertising for 13 years. The long-running Dave Thomas Campaign made Thomas one of the nation's most recognizable spokespersons. People loved him for his down-to-earth, wholesome style. He connected with people because he didn't differ greatly from the average person. And that in and of itself was unique. "From the very beginning, I never thought of myself as anybody special. And whatever I've accomplished throughout my life, when I look in the mirror, I still see myself as a hamburger cook," Thomas said.

What Skills Do I Need to Work on?

The good news is that these are all learned skills. But what do we work on first? Where do we start?

Recently, my son Shane decided that he wanted to work harder at hockey. This came after he finished the tryout for—and did not make—a select hockey team filled with some of the best kids in his age group across the country. Instead of giving up and believing he wasn't as good as all the others, he said he wanted to do better. He committed to practicing more than ever before. I was thrilled at his 12-year-old resolve! But then he asked what I think is a very wise question: "What skills do I need to work on?"

What a great question! My son immediately realized that it's not just about getting better in general, working hard, and having the desire to improve. It's about knowing *exactly* what to do and where to improve. My son and I developed a chart together that highlighted the six areas he needed to work on. He is rated on these on a scale of 1–5 by his father and coach after every game; so now Shane knows and can focus specifically on exactly what he needs to improve.

Truth be told, immediately after Shane found out he didn't make the team, he was ready to hang up his skates. He told me that he obviously wasn't any good and now that he didn't make this team, his hockey career was over. "I'll never get into a college to play hockey, the NHL is out!" Shane moaned. "It's over!"

Now, this is just a typical 12-year-old's reaction, of course. Or is it? His career and life are far from over. They scouted and hand-picked the best players in the country for the tryout. Only 17 kids made the team. He just wasn't in the top 10 percent on the day he tried out. It just depends on how you look at it.

But it really is the same for any skill you may want to improve on, including your connector skills, no matter where you think you are at the moment. If you believe that being a better connector will truly help you in business, sales, and overall success (which of course it will!), then what can be done to take action?

The worksheet that I put together with Shane is a very measurable way of assessing improvement. But the key is that we've been using this type of simple worksheet at Red Zone marketing with top sales professionals and entrepreneurs for years with measurable results! My opinion is if it works for some of the most successful sales

Figure 4.1 Red Zone Connector Weekly Skill Assessment

Skills: Ranked Each Week on a Scale of 1 to 5 (5 = Best)	"What's In It For Them" Focus	Active Listening	Asking Good Questions (so I can Listen!)	Get the Sale to Close Itself	Creating a Memorable Experience for Others	Total (25 possible)	Weekly Grade
Week 1	3	2	4	2	4	15	60
Week 2	4	5	5	3	4	21	84
Week 3						0	0
Week 4						0	0
Week 5						0	0
Week 6						0	0
Week 7						0	0
Week 8						0	0
Week 9						0	0
Week 10						0	0
Week 11						0	0

professionals in the world and it also stands the test of my pre-teen son, then it is probably fairly user friendly. But the real benefit to this is that it is simple, measurable, and visual. Create your own.

You can also access a free download of this worksheet "Red Zone Connector Skill Assessment" at www.redzonemarketing.com/The Connectors. Enter keycode "CONNECT" to download it for free!

Playing in the Red Zone

One of the client companies with whom we've been working for more than 10 years has a CEO who frequently uses a common phrase with me—sometimes more than I'd like. This CEO has achieved great personal and business successes. But every time we implement a marketing strategy, hold an event, or run a television advertisement, he comes back to me and says, "Maribeth, how can we make it better!"

I used to think to myself, "How can we make it better? Are you kidding me?" We have actually had incredible successes in the implementation of marketing strategies with this firm, and have been with them as they became a leader in their industry. Yet he questions me every time! He says it's because he knows that everything that his firm does can get a little bit better—at the least. And he doesn't want to miss the opportunity to improve.

The CEO once said to me tongue in cheek, "If this company is as good as it can possibly get, if our strategies are perfect, if I am as good as I can be, then let's close the doors and I'll retire, cause it ain't ever going to be better."

I've learned a lot from him. He plays in the Red Zone and constantly wants to get just a little bit better and score a little more often when most people don't. Admittedly, I myself am not personally driven every minute of every day to improve on everything —, but I certainly know I can always get better.

In the next section, we will discuss more in depth the five traits that most of the successful businesspeople we've studied possess. Get ready to get just a little bit better and CONNECT!

How Do They Do It? The 5 Traits of Connectors

Develop a True "What's in It for Them" Mentality

Focusing on Others Brings More for You

The most attractive people in the world are the ones who are interested in others—turned outward in cheerfulness, kindness, appreciation, instead of turned inward to be constantly centered in themselves.

Pat Boone

As I mentioned in Chapter 4, our natural instinct is to think of ourselves first. This is likely how the phrase "What's in it for me?" became so popular; we are consciously and subconsciously asking these questions all the time:

How do I appear?

How will this affect me?

How will this make me feel?

How am I feeling now?

Is this important to me?

Should I care?

The extreme of being self-focused is a condition called narcissism. The definition of narcissism, according to Merriam-Webster Dictionary, is "Excessive preoccupation with self and lack of empathy for others." A person with this disorder has a grandiose sense of self-importance and a preoccupation with fantasies of success, power, and achievement. The essential characteristic of this disorder is an exaggerated sense of self-importance that is reflected in a wide variety of situations, a sense of self-worth that in fact exceeds the individual's actual accomplishments.

While it's true that most of us aren't narcissists, this question remains: How focused are we, really, on the other people in our lives? There are all sorts of instances in business that show a lack of compassion for others. On the other hand, concentrating on others' needs can be extremely beneficial; you can assume that almost everyone else's focus is "What's in it for me," and not vice-versa. Therefore, adopting a "What's in it for them" mentality will actually allow you to stand out in a crowd, in a small group, and with your friends and neighbors. When you make it all about the other person it is exactly in line with what they want too!

Bringing People with You by Making It about Them

It's the most famous bicycle race in the world. It began more than a century ago, and has been held every year since then, except during World Wars I and II. For most of its history, it was dominated by Europeans. In fact, more than eight decades would pass before the Tour de France would be won by a non-European.

When it finally happened, the winner was an American, who would go on to win it again, and yet again—despite having to conquer serious and potentially life-threatening physical ailments. *Sports Illustrated* once named him its "Sportsman of the Year," the first time it had ever so honored a cyclist.

By now, you may have assumed that the man we've been talking about is Lance Armstrong. But it isn't! No, the man whose feats we've described is Greg LeMond. After finishing third in 1984 and second in 1985, LeMond won the 1986 race. Then, just two months before he was to defend his title, he was badly wounded in a shotgun accident that, combined with surgeries for appendicitis and tendonitis, kept him from competing for two years.

Then, in 1989—still carrying more than three dozen shotgun pellets in his body—LeMond again entered the Tour de France, but without any expectation of winning. Remarkably, over the course of this three-week event that covered more than 2,000 miles, he went on to win by a margin of eight seconds, the closest finish in tour history. In 1990, he won for the third time, but additional health complications forced him to retire from racing in 1992. His victories brought him only limited and short-lived acclaim, and even many cycling fans today would probably have a difficult time remembering his name.

Despite many similarities in their stories, LeMond never achieved the fame that was showered upon Lance Armstrong, who would win the Tour de France a record seven times—in a row—after overcoming a life-threatening bout with testicular cancer that eventually metastasized to his brain and lungs. Like LeMond, Armstrong would be named "Sportsman of the Year" by *Sports Illustrated* for his amazing achievements in this storied event.

Clearly, the accomplishments of Armstrong overshadow those of his countryman, but what was it that had this entire nation following the 2005 Tour de France with a passion normally reserved for a World Series or Super Bowl? Somehow, without even trying to do so, Armstrong had managed to bring millions of people along with him on his quest for victory.

How Do You Make Something That's about You about Others?

Armstrong undoubtedly participated in the Tour de France first and foremost for himself and his own accomplishment, determination, and will to win. But he has a particular, remarkable quality—one that we can use every day in business—that even when your goals and actions are about you, you can still make them about others, and you can do so by engaging people on a personal level. This is truly a secret to success. Most businesses have profitability and other revenue-related goals around which their firms revolve. But when we can spread our goals—and, hopefully, our achievements—to others, we will have truly reached a higher level of leadership and, ultimately, business success. And it happens most often when we can impact others personally.

When was the last time you shared something personal about yourself that caused another individual to feel personally connected to you? When I speak to groups of businesspeople, I occasionally talk about my family to make a point about making choices. I share my constant struggle to balance what my children need and what my work requires. Sometimes, I make the right choices, but sometimes I don't. When I share these specific stories, other parents immediately connect with me. I can tell because of the emotion with which they respond to these accounts. From time to time, I actually see tears in their eyes; other times, they laugh at our common situations. They will often wait until after my presentation to speak with me one on one about their own stories on family balance. They ask about other services we provide. They often buy books. I know that they feel differently about me when I share something with which they can personally identify.

Our Love of the Underdog

Although Americans love winning, I believe that we love it when the underdog wins even more. We may not want to cheer for perfect people and perfect businesses because flaws are real, and we identify with people who have them. We root for those who face the same challenges that we do—like we did with Lance Armstrong and his cancer. We all know someone with cancer. We all believe that there will be a cure and hope that we will overcome the destruction of cancer. Armstrong touched us because we felt his pain personally; we loved him for what he was doing, and we acted because of it. We even wanted to bike like Lance; bicycle sales shot up dramatically all across America. We had renewed energy to fight cancer, and we bought the yellow bracelets to give and show our commitment to the cause. We cheered because it was about overcoming cancer and ultimately about overcoming odds. In a way, Armstrong's struggles and accomplishments were about *us*!

I've been a sports fan nearly all my life, but I had absolutely no interest in cycling until Armstrong came along. His ride and story touched me—and millions of other people—in a way that few athletes ever had.

Connecting Is Not for Lone Rangers

With so much of the media spotlight focused on the day-to-day progress of individual competitors during the three weeks of the Tour de France, it's easy to lose sight of the fact that it is, in fact, a *team* event. Each year, approximately 20 teams of nine riders each compete in the event, and no individual rider—not Lance Armstrong, not Greg LeMond, not any of the four Europeans who each won five times—could possibly have achieved victory without the support and cooperation of his teammates.

In his 2000 biography, *It's Not About the Bike: My Journey Back to Life*, Armstrong described the vital role that teammates play. Some ride on ahead, clearing a path for the team leader through the enormous crowds that line the race route. Others may form a protective ring around him and, on windy days, ride directly in front of him shielding him from the wind. Armstrong wrote: "Every team needs guys who are sprinters, guys who are climbers, guys willing to do the dirty work. You don't win a road race all on your own."

In its review of Armstrong's book, the Denver-based *Rocky Mountain News* wrote: "Armstrong's book is both inspiring and entertaining . . . and he doesn't forget to thank the good people who helped him most along the way."

There's a whole lot more to the Lance Armstrong story than his victory over cancer or his achievements as a long-distance cyclist.

In 1997, two years *before* he won his first Tour de France or became a world-renowned athlete, Armstrong launched the Lance Armstrong Foundation. Its mission is to help others in their fight against cancer. In 2004, a yellow bracelet, called LIVE**STRONG**^{TM}, was designed as a fundraising tool, and by January 2006, more than 57 million of them had been purchased at $1 each.

According to the foundation's web site, www.livestrong.org, millions of dollars have been spent on cancer education and research and in the development of cancer survivorship centers across the United States. In addition, 500 cancer survivors and caregivers per month receive direct support, and an average of 200,000 web site visitors a month discover valuable tools and information about the dreaded disease of cancer.

Armstrong really brought others with him, including his team, and isn't that exactly what great leaders must do to reach higher levels of success in business? Bill Gates did not act alone. Jack Welch did not act alone. Even Donald Trump did not act alone. They needed to and successfully connected with others.

What Really Counts

We may never have the opportunity to impact as many lives as Lance Armstrong has, but we do have the opportunity, day in and day out, to make an impact on others—our clients, business colleagues, and those with whom we come in contact during our daily routines. The key is in that one little word: *others*! Ask yourself: Do I make it a point to show the others in my life that they're important to me? That I care about them? That they really matter to me?

We've often heard the expression "People don't care how much you know until they know how much you care." The main reason for its popularity and familiarity is because it's so true. Whether its meaning lies in the context of family, friendships, or business, the success or failure of the relationships we develop hinge on how well or how poorly we respond to the question "Do I matter to you?" and how we demonstrate it.

One woman who rose from abject poverty to business fame and enormous wealth did so by showing others how much they mattered. Her life's philosophy and her secret of success was "Pretend that every single person you meet has a sign around his or her neck that says, 'Make me feel important.' Not only will you succeed in sales, you will succeed in life."

At the time of her death in 2001, the company she'd founded had more than 300,000 representatives in some three dozen countries around the world, and generated annual sales in excess of $1 billion. Mary Kay Ash, who began her life with nothing, achieved fame and fortune because of her concern for others. "My goal," she had said more than once, "is to live my life in such a way that when I die, someone can say 'she cared.'" In 1980, after losing her husband to cancer, she launched the Mary Kay Ash Foundation, which is committed to funding research projects to help rid the world of cancer. Even after her death, her desire to show others that she cared about them continues through the work of her foundation.

Mary Kay didn't discover some brand-new principle; she simply applied one that has existed for centuries—one that, despite its simplicity, is so often overlooked or ignored. We don't have to launch a charitable foundation, as Mary Kay Ash and Lance Armstrong did, to show how much we care. After all, as author of the best-selling book *When Bad Things Happen to Good People,* Rabbi Harold Kushner reminds us: "The qualities that make us human emerge only in the ways we relate to other people."

It's a formula that can change our lives and the lives of those around us.

Seriously, Do I Matter to YOU?

As an active member of National Speakers Association for many years, I make it a point to attend the annual conferences each summer. One of the conference features is a program for young people, and in 2005, I took my 10-year-old daughter Elizabeth with me to Atlanta. At the opening youth session, which parents are encouraged to attend, the speaker, Andy Hickman, wore a button on his jacket with the initials "DIMTY," and asked if anyone in the audience knew what those letters stood for.

A girl from the back of the room shouted out that she knew the correct answer. She said, "Do I matter to you?"

Hickman then pointed out that we're all wearing that button—all the time. In a world where so many people seem to be wearing a "WIIFM" button ("What's in it for me?), we need to reassure those people who are important to us—in our families, in our social lives, and in our business lives—that they do indeed matter to us.

No matter what our state in life may be, and no matter how many possessions we have, we're a needy people. In the words of author Frank A. Clark, "A baby is born with a need to be loved—and never outgrows it." Along with the built-in need to be loved come such basics as the need to breathe, the need for food, clothing, and shelter, and the need for sleep.

Even when we've grown to the point where we can provide many of these basic, or physiological, needs for ourselves, other needs surface. They include a need for safety and security, for belonging and acceptance, for recognition and respect, for purpose and fulfillment.

The seeds of greatness are sown in our lives when we begin to turn from our own needs and, recognizing the needs of others, often so much greater than our own, we begin listening for the sound of their voices, asking "Do I matter to you?" In working to satisfy the needs of others, and to place those needs above our own, we're answering that vitally important question with an emphatic "Yes!"

Strategies for Making It All about Others— and Becoming Likeable at the Same Time

1. Welcoming Demeanor

The fact is that we generally like people who show they like us. There are certain behaviors that put people at ease and let others know you are interested in them—both from near and far. This welcoming element is communicated verbally through kind and welcoming words and also non-verbally by the upbeat, positive energy you give off, your facial expressions (smiling, looking at the other person), and your general demeanor (e.g., posture, handshakes, hugs, close distance.)

2. Relevance to the Other Person

Relevance has to do with the degree to which you express interest in another person's interests and needs. When you show genuine interest in someone's passion or their needs, you create a bond. They know you are sincerely interested in them. Therefore, asking questions such as "What's the biggest challenge you face in your business?" or "How is your training for the marathon going?" shows them you are concerned with things that may be important to them.

Perhaps even more powerful is demonstrating a deep common interest, such as being actively involved in a charity or cause that you both care about. That type of relevance can have even more of an impact in shaping another's perception about you. It tells the other person that you are a lot like them, and they want you to be a lot like them.

3. Empathy

Empathy consists of your ability to "put yourself in the other's shoes," to identify with them, understand how they feel, and appreciate the situation they're in. You know them in important ways, and they feel that you know. Additionally, when you develop a sense of who they are without judgment, they feel accepted just as they are. Being an empathetic person says a lot about your ability to connect with others.

4. Authenticity

People who are authentic, genuine, and real are usually at ease because they're not trying to cover anything up. In turn, their being at ease puts others at ease. Authenticity is giving others the idea that what you see is what you get. Real people are easy to be around because you feel safe knowing that you can trust what they say.

In sales, less of the memorized pitch and more of the informal conversational approach is exceptionally more successful. Wouldn't you want to buy from someone you could really believe was giving you things as they truly are? No pretense, no fluffing up the facts—true authenticity.[1]

Everyday Greatness

For more than 80 years, *Reader's Digest*, which has the largest circulation of any magazine in the world, has featured story after story about individuals who have placed the needs of others above their own, often at great personal sacrifice. Recently, 63 of those stories, compiled by David K. Hatch, were published in a book aptly titled *Everyday Greatness* (Rutledge Hill Press, 2006).

In addition to the stories, the book features numerous insights, reflections and running commentary by Stephen R. Covey, author of several best-selling books, including the immensely popular one, *The 7 Habits of Highly Effective People*, which has sold more than 15 million copies worldwide.

Covey also wrote an extensive introduction to *Everyday Greatness*, in which he describes that kind of greatness as having to do with "character and contribution, as distinguished from 'secondary greatness,' which has to do with wealth, fame, prestige, or position. Everyday Greatness is a way of living, not a one-time event. . . . It speaks more about people's motives than about their talents; more about small and simple deeds than about grandiose accomplishments. It is humble."

On the topic of humility, the well-known 19th century author, poet, and artist John Ruskin wrote this: "I believe that the first test of a truly great man is his humility. Really great men have a curious feeling that the greatness is not in them but through them."

People who are wearing that DIMTY button exist all around us. If you're going to show them they really do matter to you—that you're ready and willing to stand with them and help meet their needs—it will mean humbling yourself and placing their interests above your own. That's the true path to greatness: It lies not *in* you but *through* you.

Business Alliances—It is All about the Other Person

When networking and formal and informal strategic business alliances truly work, it is because they are profitable for both parties. When these methods *don't* work, it is usually because they are not mutually profitable. It is a simple fact in business.

I have heard many accounts from businesspeople about how they have often been on the short end of a business relationship like this. They gave significant referrals, but received nothing in return. Now, there could be many reasons for this failure to connect. But think of it this way: If you refer business to others as a constant practice in your daily life, will you ultimately be better or worse off for it? My belief is that the more you give, the more you get. Yes, sometimes making it more about the other businessperson will backfire on us or won't be equal. A majority of the time, however, it will most likely turn out to be quite favorable, and it is how many businesspeople have found success.

Downloadable Form 5.1: "The What's in It for *Them* FACTOR"

In individual interactions you have, do you think . . .

1. I wonder how this will affect him/her?
   Always   Often   Sometimes   Never

2. How will this make them feel?
   Always   Often   Sometimes   Never

3. Will he/she really care?
   Always   Often   Sometimes   Never

4. Is this interesting to him/her?
   Always   Often   Sometimes   Never

5. Does this really matter?
   Always   Often   Sometimes   Never

6. Am I communicating effectively so he/she clearly understands what I am saying?
   Always   Often   Sometimes   Never

7. Have I made the other person feel better after interacting with me?
   Always   Often   Sometimes   Never

8. Have I reached out to someone I don't know today to give them something they need?
   Always   Often   Sometimes   Never

You can also access a free download of "The What's In It For Them FACTOR" at www.redzonemarketing.com/TheConnectors. Enter keycode "CONNECT" to download it for free!

In Other Words

People will forget what you said; people will forget what you did; but people will never forget how you made them feel.

Anonymous

The best way to find yourself is to lose yourself in the service of others.
Mohandas K. Gandhi

Life is an exciting business, and most exciting when it is lived for others.
Helen Keller

A little consideration, a little thought for others, makes all the difference.
A.A. Milne

CHAPTER
6

Listen! Curiously Listen

Most of the successful people I've known are the ones who do more listening than talking.

—Bernard M. Baruch

E very summer, we have an old-fashioned block party in our neighborhood where we close off the street and just have a good time, with lots of food, fun and games for the kids. A few years ago, I was standing in the food line next to a neighbor named Amy. I hadn't seen her in months and barely knew her, but it was obvious she'd lost a lot of weight. I mentioned to her that I noticed she lost weight and told her she looked great. Amy responded that she actually had lost 40 pounds. Wow! I was intrigued! So I began asking her a lot of questions about how she lost the weight, what diet it was, what she was eating, her exercise regimen, and so on. I wanted to know everything, because I was very curious about how she did it. We spent about 10 minutes together where she told me exactly what she did to lose the weight including the changes she made in her eating habits and the exercises she was doing. She even told me about how her husband was responding to this weight loss!

Later that afternoon, another neighbor at the block party shared with me that she was just talking with Amy and that Amy was telling her how much she liked me. Me? That was surprising; I hadn't said a word to Amy about myself. She didn't really know me or anything about me, my business, my kids, my house, my husband—nothing. I simply was curious and asked a lot of questions and listened to her interesting story of weight loss—a topic that was very important to her. In thinking about it, I believe Amy expressed that she liked me because I listened to her, not because I talked. In fact, if I would have talked about me at all I assume that she would only have liked me less!

Curiously Listening

Although it is almost counterintuitive, we may not need to impress others with stories about ourselves and our accomplishments. It may not be logical, but the reality of human nature is that if you're genuinely curious and really listen to a person, he or she equates that to caring. It is unique and immediately sets the listener apart. Great businessman Walt Disney credited curiosity for much of his success. "We're curious," he said, "and curiosity keeps leading us down new paths."

Many successful businesspeople, no matter what product or service they're representing, are genuinely and transparently curious. Once they uncover what their prospects and clients really value, they won't have to sell anything—the sale will close itself! So let's first go in depth on listening, and then we will get to asking great questions next.

Good Listening Skills Bring Success in Business

Several years ago, there was actually a public service announcement that ran on television on this topic. It talked about the importance of good listening skills and the difference between hearing and listening. It explained that hearing is a physical ability, while listening is a skill. Listening skills allow one to make sense of and understand what another person is saying. In other words, listening skills allow you to understand what someone is talking about.

In 1991, the United States Department of Labor Secretary's Commission on Achieving Necessary Skills (SCANS) identified five competencies and three foundation skills that are essential for those entering the workforce. Listening skills were among the foundation skills SCANS identified.

Good listening skills make workers more productive; the ability to listen carefully allows us to:

- better understand assignments and what is expected of us;
- build rapport with coworkers, bosses, and clients;
- show support;
- work better in a team-based environment;
- resolve problems with customers, coworkers, and bosses;
- answer questions; and
- find underlying meanings in what others say.

In other words, listening is the first step in truly connecting with others.

Can Listening Save You from Getting Sued?

How important is listening? In his best-selling book *Blink*, Malcolm Gladwell tells the amazing story of a study conducted by a medical researcher to determine the likelihood of doctors being sued by their patients. According to Gladwell, "Roughly half of the doctors had never been sued. The other half had been sued at least twice." The research disclosed specific differences between the two groups. "The surgeons who had never been sued," Gladwell reported, "spent more than three minutes longer with each patient than those who had been sued did."

What took place during those extra three minutes some of the doctors spent with their patients? They allowed time for questions and encouraged their patients to talk. They paid attention, and they listened. They showed that they cared.

If a patient's procedure went awry, however, someone did get sued. But in the case of these "listening surgeons," it was someone else and not them. In documented cases, it was usually the internist or radiologist that that patient brought a lawsuit against. Why? Because they actually liked the *surgeon*, and we don't sue people we like!

The Effects of Curious Listening Can Be Dramatic!

Being a good listener has enormous advantages. Consider this statement by contemporary American educator and author John J. DiGaetani: "The effects of really good listening can be dramatic. These effects include the satisfied customer who will come back, the contented employee who will stay with the company, the manager who has the trust of his staff, and the salesman who tops his quota."

An accurate statement to be sure, but not exactly surprising. The importance of listening has been recognized throughout recorded history. "Know how to listen," advised Plutarch, a first century Greek historian and writer. Some 1,500 years later, Shakespeare offered similar advice: "Give every man thine ear, but few thy voice."

Shortly after the dawning of the nineteenth century, Revolutionary War veteran John Marshall, who had also served in Congress and as U.S. Secretary of State, was appointed Chief Justice of the U.S. Supreme Court. He held that post for nearly 35 years, longer than any other person, and was known for both his unswerving integrity and his brilliance and eloquence in communicating on legal and constitutional issues. Marshall knew well the importance of listening. He once commented that "Listening well is as powerful a means of communication and influence as to talk well."

The Lost Art

However, despite almost universal and historic agreement on its importance, listening still seems to be largely a lost art, perhaps more so than ever in this busy, hectic, and instant-everything world of ours. We may hear what others are saying to us, but are we really listening? "Most people never listen," wrote Ernest Hemingway, and Thomas Merton declared it to be "obsolete."

In fact, one study involved asking participants to list the characteristics of the worst listeners they know. These characteristics included:

- always interrupts
- jumps to conclusions
- finishes my sentences
- changes the subject
- is impatient
- loses his/her temper
- fidgets nervously
- fails to maintain eye contact
- climbs on a soapbox to demonstrate how much he/she knows about a subject

American author and editor Edgar Watson Howe pretty well summed it up when he wrote, "No man would listen to you talk if he didn't know it was his turn next."

What Does It Mean to Really Listen?

Curious listening is an active process that is comprised of three basic steps.

1. **Hearing the Essence.** Hearing just means listening enough to catch what the speaker is saying. In a very simplistic example,

a financial advisor may listen to a client speak about her two grown children and how she wants to gift them money. If you can repeat the fact back, then you have heard what has been said.

2. **Getting It.** The next part of curiously listening happens when you take what you have heard and understand it in your own way. In the example of the discussion with your client and her children, think about what that might mean. You might think, "Maybe she wants to give her children money right now?"

3. **Confirmation.** Even if you are sure that you understand what the speaker has said, don't assume that you know what he/she *means*. This client may have wanted to leave money to the children in her will, she may want to create a trust, or she may want to do it right now. Ask questions to confirm any and all assumptions you have and then think about whether it makes sense. Do you believe what you have heard? Ask more questions until you have confirmed it in your mind that you have heard the client correctly and understand all of what she means.

There's Something about the Way That a Curious Listener Makes Us Feel

Curious listening is a structured listening-and-questioning technique, which helps you develop and enhance relationships through a stronger understanding of what is being conveyed both intellectually and emotionally. But it's also what a great listener *doesn't* say that is so powerful. Have you ever been around someone who just wants to listen to you, wants to hear all about your day, or your recent trip? Someone who is truly interested in you. Hmmm. I don't think you find them very often. But when you do, they really stick out. The act of listening shows that you care.

An example of this is an entrepreneur with whom I have worked who runs a multimillion-dollar data architecture firm. He is so skilled at listening that when I first met him, it was almost uncomfortable. He gives such unwavering eye contact, and his body language conveys his complete interest in everything that another person is saying. It certainly isn't typical. But since he started his firm when he was 20 years old, he's constantly been engaging in investigative-type work to find out technical solutions for his clients. He does it by listening intently to hear all the things the client has to say. And he says that often the client already has the solution if you listen hard enough for it.

This concentrated listening has served him well both personally and professionally. It is his unique ability to pay unwavering attention to the person he's with that allows him to connect with others on a different level, be memorable and likeable, and ultimately make almost twice the number of sales than most of his competitors in the United States.

If someone wants to listen to what you have to say, then he or she must be a good person and, simply, someone you'd like to do business with.

Listening for the Remarkable

"Find the remarkable in conversations with others," said Sunny Bates, an entrepreneur who maintains a network of some of the most prominent people in the world. "There is *always* something that a person says in every conversation that is truly remarkable."

Bates sits on the boards of many organizations and foundations and is also on the advisory board for the Ted Conference that gathers the world's leading thinkers and doers together each year. Bates says that it doesn't matter if the person is prominent, famous, or just an everyday person. The key is to listen and remember the remarkable. "I always listen for the remarkable and then repeat it back in future communications. It shows you are really listening and remembering."

Think about the remarkable things that people say to you. Record them in your mind (and of course your database). You may be amazed at the reaction you get when you repeat these things back in your subsequent conversation. The result may be that the relationship itself that you have with that other person may become more remarkable!

Lee Iacocca Says Listening Curiously is #1 Trait of Leaders

After working at Ford for 32 years, Lee Iacocca joined Chrysler in 1978 to become CEO and eventual hero and legendary leader. Soon after coming to Chrysler, Iacocca realized that the company was in a state of emergency, and so he had to make some drastic decisions. He had to fire many of the executives. He tried to set up a partnership between Chrysler and Volkswagen, but Volkswagen realized how deep in debt Chrysler was and the deal fell through. Eventually, Iacocca was forced to go to the government to ask for government-backed loans. He also bargained with the union for cuts in salary and benefits. He reduced his salary to $1 per year to show that everyone at the company must be willing to sacrifice if their company was to survive. He was able to understand the worker as well as the executives and somehow pull them together. By 1983, Chrysler was back on its feet, and on July 13, 1983, Chrysler paid back all its government loans. Lee made a public statement, "We at Chrysler borrow money the old-fashioned way. We pay it back."

Iacocca has credited listening as a key element to his success. In his book *Where Have All the Leaders Gone?* (Simon & Schuster 2007), Iacocca says, "A leader has to show curiosity. He has to listen to people outside of the 'Yes, sir' crowd in his inner circle. Businesspeople need to listen at least as much as they need to talk. Too many people fail to realize that real communication goes in both directions."

In a speech to the employees of Chrysler on June 26, 2008, when he was being recognized with a Lifetime Achievement Award, Iacocca discussed strategies for right now. In reviewing the challenges that Chrysler has undergone on and off for 50 years, he said to the employees, "Stick together. When you don't understand something, be curious. Ask questions. The first trait of good leaders is curiosity. Ask questions and listen."

Thinking Fast—But Not Talking Too Quickly

In business, sometimes we feel that we have to move so fast. But when you're communicating with others, it's always best to take your time. Thoughts move about four times as fast as speech. With practice, you will be able to listen carefully and simultaneously think about what you are hearing, really understand it, and give feedback to the person who is speaking.

The way to become a better listener is to practice active listening. This occurs when you make a conscious effort to hear not only the words that another person is saying but, more importantly, to try and understand the total message being sent—taking their inflection, emotion, and physical gestures into account as well. To do this you must pay attention to the other person very carefully. You cannot allow yourself to become distracted by what else may be going on around you or by forming counter arguments that you'll make when the other person stops speaking. Nor can you allow yourself to lose focus on what the other person is saying. All of these barriers contribute to a lack of listening and understanding.

Good Listeners Listen with Their Faces

One skill that some of the most successful people employ is that to be a good listener, you must *act like a good listener*. We have worked hard our entire lives trying to tune out all of the information that hits us during every minute of every day. It is therefore important to change our physical body language from someone who is trying to get away from receiving information to someone who wants to receive it. In essence, our faces say it all.

Another skill is to visually listen. Your eyes pick up the non-verbal signals that all people send out when they are speaking. By looking at the speaker, your eyes will also complete the eye contact that speakers are trying to make. A speaker will work harder at sending out the information when they see a receptive listener. Your eyes help fulfill the communication circuit that must be established between speaker and listener.

Your face must also move and give the range of emotions that indicate whether you are following what the speaker is saying. By moving your face with the conversation, you can better concentrate on what the person is saying. Your face actively captures information.

Can You Top This?

Many years ago during the heyday of radio, a popular program was a panel show called *Can You Top This?* to which listeners would submit their favorite jokes. Selected jokes would be recited over the airwaves, and the three panelists—all well-known comedians of the time—would each tell a joke on the same subject. The amount of the contestant's prize depended on how many of the comedians "topped" the submitted joke, based on the level of audience laughter.

That show long since faded into oblivion, but the game goes on—and it's no laughing matter. If we mention our latest illness, the person we're talking with has always been sicker. Our report of a pleasant week at the beach is immediately topped by a lengthy spiel about a month-long holiday in the Swiss Alps. And it makes no difference if it happened 20 or 30 years ago. If we made or lost money on an investment, the one to whom we mention it lost or made even more. And so it goes. The game continues with everyone talking and no one listening. Even late, great comedian Groucho Marx, who built his reputation on his wisecracking interruptions, eventually figured out the importance of listening. "Years ago," he said, "I tried to top everybody, but I don't anymore.

I realized it was killing conversation. When you're always trying for a topper, you aren't really listening. It ruins communication."

I'm Listening to You

To enhance your listening skills, the person with whom you're conversing needs to know that you are listening to what he or she is saying, not focusing on yourself, and wants to see how you will contribute to the conversation. To understand the importance of this, ask yourself if you've ever been engaged in a conversation when you wondered if the other person was listening to what you were saying. You questioned if your message was getting across or if it was even worthwhile to continue speaking. It can feel like talking to a brick wall, and I believe it's something we all want to avoid.

Acknowledgement can be something as simple as a nod of the head or a simple "uh-huh." You aren't necessarily agreeing with the person; you are merely indicating that you are listening. Using body language and other signs to demonstrate you are listening also reminds you to pay attention and not let your mind wander. When you're finding it particularly difficult to concentrate on what someone is saying, try repeating their words mentally as they say it—this will reinforce their message and help you control mind drift.

You should also try to respond to the speaker in a way that will encourage him or her to continue speaking, so that you can get the information that you need. While nodding and uh-huhing says you're interested, an occasional question or comment to recap what has been said communicates that you understand the message as well.

Seven Simple Yet Powerful Listening Tips

1. **Full Attention.** Give your full attention to the person who is speaking. Don't look at your computer or BlackBerry, or gaze somewhere else.

2. **Focus.** Make sure your mind is focused on the person in front of you—if only for a short period of time. If you feel your mind wandering, change the position of your body and try to concentrate on the speaker's words.

3. **Don't Interrupt.** Let the other person finish before you begin to talk. Speakers appreciate having the chance to say everything they would like to say without being interrupted. When you interrupt with your comments it feels to the other person like you aren't listening, even if you really are. And you can't truly listen if you're busy thinking about what you want say next.

4. **Pay Special Attention to the Key Points.** The main ideas are the most important points a person wants to get across. They may be mentioned at the start or end or they may be repeated a number of times.

5. **Watch for Non-Verbal Cues.** A good listener knows that being attentive to what the speaker *doesn't* say is as important as being attentive to what he/she does say. Look for non-verbal cues such as facial expressions and posture to get the full gist of what the speaker is telling you.

6. **Ask Questions.** Ask questions to clarify what the person who is talking is saying. Repeat what they have said in your own words so you can be sure your understanding is correct.

7. **Respond.** Sit up straight, look directly at the person talking, and occasionally lean in to the conversation. Nod to show with your body that you are listening. Also give verbal acknowledgements ("yes" or "Hmmm" or "I see") to show that you hear what they are saying.

Time Spent Listening

Upon observing the most successful financial advisors with whom we work, there is a key similarity relating to how they listen. To further enhance our observation, we formally surveyed some of the top advisors in the country and asked them what percentage of each client or prospect meeting is spent listening and what percentage is spent talking.

For the advisors who make more than $1,000,000 per year, it is almost unanimous: They spend at least 50 percent of the time listening in every meeting they attend. But the most significant fact is that in the very first meeting they have with a person—wherein they are attempting to secure this individual as a new client— they are spending a majority of the time listening, not talking. One might assume that during that first meeting, the financial advisor would be tempted to go into great detail about all of the wonderful things that their business offers, how much knowledge they have, and how they can provide help. But instead of making the clients' wants needs and challenges an afterthought, these executives identify this aspect as the primary focus of the meeting. They allow it to determine the amount of time that they were allowed and encouraged to talk about other matters. This seems almost the opposite of what most salespeople do in the first meeting, and it is probably one of the major reasons behind these top-earning advisors' success.

A Nation of Non-Listeners

The late Steve Allen, host of television's original *Tonight Show*, frequently involved his audiences in experiments designed to be humorous but that also demonstrated what poor listeners we all tend to be. Allen would go out into the audience and whisper a brief statement to someone sitting in an aisle seat. That person was then asked to whisper the same statement to the next person, with the process continuing all across the row. The person seated in the last seat of the row was asked to repeat into the microphone what he or she had heard.

At the same time, the original statement was flashed on the screen. Invariably, the disparity was enormous and always resulted in great laughter. But, the sobering point it made, night after night, was that we're a nation of non-listeners. That was in the mid-1950s, and a half-century later, it's still a fairly popular form of amusement when friends gather for a relaxing evening of fun and games. And there's no evidence to suggest we've become any better at listening today than we were then.

An Acquired Skill

Although listening is a skill that can be learned, very little has ever been done about teaching it. As children, we began tuning out our parents, and as we grew, we applied that same technique to our teachers and pastors. So, it's little wonder that, by the time we began to make our way in the world, we didn't listen to our boss or our coworkers, our customers or prospects—or they to us! Not only weren't we taught *how* to listen, we were never taught the *importance* of listening.

Here's an interesting fact: The six letters that make up the word "listen" can be rearranged to make up another word that's essential if we're to be good listeners—"silent." By your silence, you're conveying to the speaker this message: "You matter to me." To strengthen your connections in business, the strongest building block you can use is your ability to listen quietly and carefully. As the late Dean Rusk, U.S. Secretary of State under presidents John F. Kennedy and Lyndon B. Johnson, noted: "One of the best ways to persuade others is with your ears—by listening to them."

We're probably all familiar with the old adage that the reason God gave us two ears but only one mouth is so that we'd do twice as much listening as talking. Yet, we've somehow come to believe that talking is the way to impress others, so they'll recognize how smart we are, how much we know, and what we can do for them.

But it takes more than just our ears to make us good listeners. It also takes eye contact. In the words of author and poet Martin Buxbaum, "It's just as important to listen to someone with your eyes as it is with your ears." Indeed, it's very difficult to convince the person who's talking that you're paying attention to what he or she is saying if you're looking at someone or something else or gazing off into space.

The Listening Stick

Many years ago, a communications consultant named Ben Joyce designed and copyrighted a simple but effective system called The Listening Stick. It included a small wooden stick, with the words "Please, will you listen to me?" printed on one side and "Thank you" on the other. It came with an "Owner's Manual," a brochure with detailed instructions on how to become a better listener, and a business-card size "Quick Use Guide," explaining how to use The Listening Stick. "If you listen, you can learn," said Joyce. Or, to put it conversely, if you're talking, you're not learning.

Joyce added: "Really good listeners are givers. They give respect, attention, time, patience, trust, understanding and support. When you really listen, you are allowing the other person to simply talk without effort or distraction. You do not create a need to struggle. Very good listeners develop very good relationships because they create trust."

In order to build relationships, show people you care and that they matter to you, and to create trust, focus on becoming a good listener. Whatever talking you do should be pretty much limited to asking questions. When you do, listen carefully and completely to the answers you get. If they're not clear, ask for clarification and keep on listening.

Listening is not an easy skill to learn; it takes discipline and concentration. Psychiatrist and author (of books including *The Road Less Traveled*, which has been translated into nearly two dozen languages and has sold more than 20 million copies) M. Scott Peck put it this way: "You cannot truly listen to anyone and do anything else at the same time."

Become a good listener. Because so few others practice the art of listening, it's the most effective way to make lasting connections with others.

Final Reminders to Improve Listening

- If you are really listening intently, you should feel tired after your speaker has finished. Effective listening is an active rather than a passive activity.
- When you find yourself drifting away during a listening session, change your body position.
- Listen with your face.
- Contribute to the conversation first with your ears, face, and body, and finally, let them hear your voice.

Downloadable Form 6.1: "The Listening Assessment"

1. I look like I'm listening when I am.
   Always   Often   Sometimes   Never

2. I summarize what the other person has said.
   Always   Often   Sometimes   Never

3. I hear the person completely before I make judgments about the message.
   Always   Often   Sometimes   Never

4. I let the other person finish his own sentences even when he pauses.
   Always   Often   Sometimes   Never

5. I keep my eyes on the speaker's eyes.
   Always   Often   Sometimes   Never

6. I concentrate on what the person is saying, not what he or she looks like.
   Always   Often   Sometimes   Never

7. I ask questions of a speaker so I can better understand what they are saying.
   Always   Often   Sometimes   Never

8. Whether I agree with the speaker or not, I listen to all statements made.
   Always   Often   Sometimes   Never

9. I listen with my face.
   Always   Often   Sometimes   Never

10. I work on improving my empathic and active listening skills.
    Always   Often   Sometimes   Never

You can also access a free download of "The Listening Assessment" at www.redzonemarketing.com/TheConnectors. Enter keycode "CONNECT" to download it for free!

In Other Words

A good listener is a silent flatterer.

Charlie "Tremendous" Jones

Be different. . . . When word gets out that you can listen when others tend to talk, you will be treated as a sage.

Edward Koch

Then I want to sit and listen and have someone talk, tell me things. . . . Not to say anything — to listen and listen and be taught.

Anne Morrow Lindbergh

Listening is an active pursuit that requires skill and practice.

Stacey Lucas

Formula for handling people: 1) Listen to the other person's story; 2) Listen to the other person's full story; 3) Listen to the other person's full story first.

General George C. Marshall

Sainthood emerges when you can listen to someone's tale of woe and not respond with a description of your own.

Andrew V. Mason

One friend, one person who is truly understanding, who takes the trouble to listen to us as we consider our problem, can change our whole outlook on the world.

Dr. Elton Mayo

A good listener is not only popular everywhere, but after a while he knows something.

Wilson Mizner

Nobody ever got into any trouble listening. That's about the safest thing that one can do in life. If you listen to people and you pay attention to them, then you're bound to learn.

James O'Toole

The road to the heart is the ear.

Voltaire

CHAPTER 7

Important Questions to Ask that Attract Connections

We simply can't make clear distinctions without the use of questions! No distinctions! No decisions! No actions! No wonder questions are such a powerful force. Without questions we would not—could not—take any action!

—Bobb Biehl

To curiously listen and accomplish all that listening contributes to business success, it is quite clearly critical that the other person is talking. Otherwise, there would be nothing to listen to! But how do you engage the other person and get them to begin talking? Good questions lead to good talking and, therefore, better connections. After all, according to Albert Einstein, "The important thing is not to stop questioning."

Did You Ask Any Good Questions Today?

Unless you have an interest in physics or happen to be a physicist yourself, chances are that the name Martin L. Perl will mean nothing to you. Born in New York City in 1927, Perl was the son of Jewish parents who had emigrated from Russia to the United States around the start of the twentieth century. He went on to become a distinguished physicist and, in 1995, was awarded the Nobel Prize in Physics.

When once asked to what he attributed his success, he gave the credit to his mother. "Every day when I came home from school," he explained, "she asked me, 'So, Marty, did you ask any good questions today?'"

As Perlman learned from an early age, asking good questions is one of the keys to building successful relationships. You may be conversing with your next-door neighbor, the prospective client you've just met, or the stranger you're sitting next to on an airplane, but in any and all of these cases, asking good questions means asking open-ended ones. These are the questions that require more than a simple "yes" or "no" answer. You may be surprised at how much you can learn.

Recently, a colleague shared a story with me about how effective asking these kinds of questions can be. He and his wife had invited a couple who had just moved in next door to join them and a few long-time neighbors for dessert one evening. "One lady," he said, "showed a sincere interest in all our guests by asking them questions about their backgrounds and their families. By the end of the evening, we had not only become better acquainted with the new arrivals, but, because of a few thoughtful and sincere questions, we learned a lot more about another neighbor whom we've known well, or thought we had, for five years. It was a great experience."

Asking Questions Effectively

"Garbage in, garbage out" is a popular phrase often used to describe computer technology. If you put the wrong information in, you'll get the wrong information out. This same "Garbage Principle" applies to communication in general: If you ask the wrong questions, you'll probably get the wrong answer, or at least not quite what you were hoping for.

Asking good questions is at the heart of effective communication and information exchange. By using the right questions in a particular situation, you can improve a whole range of communications skills. You can gather better information and learn more, build stronger relationships, manage people more effectively, help others to learn, and most important, create lasting connections.

All the Right Questions

Not long ago, my husband and I experienced the effectiveness of that approach in a powerful way. We had been house hunting and wound up spending more than we had planned to buy our new home, which was in a town where we had decided we didn't want to live. Had we grown tired of trying to find our dream home? Or had we succumbed to the persuasive tactics of an overaggressive realtor? No and no.

The realtor we had chosen, Wendi, never tried to sell us anything. Instead, she asked us question after question about what we were looking for, about the specific features each of us wanted in our new home, and why these were important to us. She asked us questions for almost two hours. I remember answering her questions and describing in detail what my dream kitchen would look like. A big room with lots of cabinets, a long island in the middle, a double oven, and counters everywhere. Now, I don't cook, and Wendi knew that. But because of her questioning, she found out why I wanted such a specifically designed kitchen. It's because we entertain all the time, and it often seems that people gather in the kitchen. So, I wanted my kitchen to be designed for a lot of people to gather and socialize. If Wendi hadn't asked all the questions she did, she may have just assumed that a small kitchen would be fine since she knew I didn't love to cook. The right question wasn't, "Do you like to cook?" It was, "Tell me what happens in your kitchen now?"

When Wendi called to tell us that she found our house, she was telling the truth. We took only a few steps into the house and knew it was just the place we were looking for. That's why we ended up spending more than we said we would in a town in which we originally thought we hadn't wanted to live. And it's also why Wendi was the top real estate agent in the area in sales. I didn't know that at the time, because she didn't tell me; she didn't have to. She spent her time asking us questions and not talking about herself and her qualifications. She was successful because of her patience and diligence for questioning. When you use that approach and pay attention to the answers you're getting, you don't have to establish your credibility; the work that you do for your clients does so for you.

Heart Questions

It may not be what we say to someone that affects them in a personal way, but rather how we respond to what *they* say and how they feel. If we can get to the core of an issue and hear another person express her pain or joy, we will have made a significant connection with them. If we listen and show we care about their situation without speaking, we most likely will be perceived differently and more positively. And in order to do so, we must pose questions that get to the heart of what matters most to them. Some powerful "Heart Questions" are:

- Tell me about your children.
- What were the biggest challenges you had to starting this career or business?
- What keeps you awake at night?
- What is your greatest accomplishment?
- Who are you responsible for?

Almost everyone who answers questions like these will experience some kind of emotional reaction in regards to their response. If you are asking these questions, and are authentically interested in what they have to say, then you will have jump-started a connection and a relationship that will not easily be forgotten.

Speed Up the Relationship

There are some heart questions that, if answered truthfully, can develop the relationship-building process more quickly than others. Twenty-four-year-old Canadian self-made millionaire James Timothy White attributes his ability to connect with others as a foundation of his success. He now runs a multimillion-dollar international enterprise that he began as a landscaping business he started when he was 12 with a $20 show shovel as his only piece of equipment.

One of this young entrepreneur's secrets to creating long-term connections with others is his capacity to develop a relationship with some people in the span of 30 seconds. White claims that he simply says to the other person, "Tell me something you've never told someone else." He asserts that this question has allowed him to discover all sorts of unbelievable things about people. White commits to the other person that he will forever keep it a secret—and he does. By getting these people to open up to him, White has attained an advanced level of trust and emotion. Others often say to him, "I can't believe I just told you that." However, White knows that the most important thing is that they told him, he still is there listening, and that he still likes them!

When you get to the core of a particular person through the questions you ask—and persuade them to share things that are truly important to them—you have built a bond. You've done so because you are asking, listening, interested, and empathetic. They have divulged an important piece of themselves, and you forever share a connection because of it.

Fulfilling a Dream

I began this chapter with a quote by Bobb Biehl, from his book entitled *The Question Book*. As a successful management consultant for many years, Biehl built his practice by learning to ask questions. "No problem in the world," he writes, "has ever been solved without a question or series of questions being asked first."

A colleague of mine named Bob Kelly told me about his personal experience with Biehl. It seems that Bob, a long-time banker, had moved from Florida to California to take a new job in a different field. Less than two years later, the organization he worked for ran into serious financial difficulties and his job was eliminated.

One of the first friends Bob had made in California was Bobb Biehl, and so he went to him for advice. However, instead of offering any advice, Biehl began asking questions: "What would you really love to do, Bob, if money were no object?"

Bob's responsed, "I've always dreamed of being in business for myself."

"Doing what?" Biehl asked.

"Writing and editing," Bob replied.

Biehl's next question was "Why haven't you done it?"

Bob explained, "I have a wife and kids to feed, so bringing home a salary has always been a high priority."

"Bob, you have no salary right now," Biehl pointed out, "so what's stopping you from following your dream?"

Biehl offered no advice, nor did he attempt to persuade Jim to follow a specific path. All he did was ask a series of questions, and wait for Bob to provide the answers. That's all it took for Bob to begin pursuing his dream.

Questioning Your Employees

To Jack Welch, the legendary former CEO of General Electric, business leadership is all about knowing what questions to ask of his subordinates. "That's all managing is," Welch says. "Just coming up with the right questions and getting the right answers." To understand the strategic issues within each department of GE businesses—and to see where these business units were going—Welch asked the following five strategic questions:

1. What does your global competitive environment look like?
2. In the last three years, what have your competitors done?
3. In the same period, what have you done to them?
4. How might they attack you in the future?
5. What are your plans to leapfrog over them?[1]

Based on the answers to these, Welch received all the information he needed to make decisions and help lead his team.

Questioning Your Clients

Clients will consciously and subconsciously rate you on several factors, including satisfaction, delight, service, communication, your staff, and so on. But how do you think you rate with your clients? Have you ever thought about discovering their level of satisfaction and what's really important to them about you and the business? Asking your clients what they want may be one of the best places to use your best questions. You'll make better decisions if you know all the facts.

The How-Tos of Effective Questioning

The way in which you ask questions is very important in establishing a basis for effective communication. Valuable questions open the door to knowledge and understanding, which is why it's important to:

1. Know the best questions to ask and when to ask them.
2. Do a little thinking before asking questions.
3. If possible, do research before meeting with someone so you will be able to ask the most appropriate and engaging questions.
4. Think of the type and length of answer you may want, and then formulate your questions.

As CEO of Lefora, a forum hosting service company, Paul Bragiel has run three different software and gaming companies. He says he reaches out to as many people as he can and that he's done so for years. Whenever he can, he will research the person he's planning to meet prior to their face-to-face encounter. This allows Bragiel to hone in on areas of interest, ask questions about those interests, and listen. And he certainly knows something about connecting and asking questions; Lefora has developed software that allows groups of people to create forums to ask questions, discuss, and socialize online about common topics. They currently have more than 50,000 groups and more than 1,000,000 users signed up with Lefora. (Learn more about creating a forum for connecting in Chapter 18: Connecting Through Social Media Technology.)

Choosing Questions

You ask a specific question when you want to hear a specific answer, right? Similarly, you ask open-ended questions when you want the person answering them to feel free to provide as much information as they can. Open questions are those that cannot be answered with a straight "yes" or "no," can be used to gain insight into the other person's character, and are meant to invite a response.

There comes a time in every conversation with someone you've just met when you go from "How are you?" to "*Who* are you?" A helpful technique for making this transition is by asking creative, open-ended questions, which build rapport and invite the person with whom you're communicating to share their experiences, insights, and preferences.

Open and Closed Questions

Open questions encourage the speaker to share. They elicit a more detailed response than closed questions. "What" and "why" are usually helpful starts to open questions.

A closed question usually receives a single word or very short answer. For example, "Are you tired?" brings an answer of "Yes" or "No." "Where were you born?" is generally answered with the name of a hometown.

Open questions elicit longer answers. They usually begin with what, why, or how. An open question asks the respondent for his or her knowledge, opinion, or feelings. "Tell me" and "describe" can also be used in the same way as open questions. For example:

- What happened in your meeting today?
- Why did she say that?
- How was the game?
- What happened next?
- Tell me more.

Open questions are good for developing an open conversation and finding out more detail. You can also use open questions to find out the other person's opinion or issues.

Some Sample Questions

The following, in no particular order, are samples of the kinds of open-ended questions you can ask to learn more about another person. Of course, in selling situations, for a home, a car, investments, and so on, you'll also need to ask specific questions relating to that situation.

- Tell me about yourself.
- What do you value?
- What are your short-term goals?
- What's your biggest challenge?
- What keeps you awake at night?
- What do you want and need?
- What gives you the greatest satisfaction?

- What would you do if you had unlimited time and resources?
- What do you consider your greatest accomplishment[s] to date?
- What person has had the greatest influence on you? How?
- Where would you like your life to be 10 years from now?
- What plans do you have for your retirement?
- What do you enjoy doing most in your leisure time?
- How would you like other people to perceive you?
- What traits in others do you admire most?
- What outside interests do you have?
- What's your happiest memory?
- How would you define success?
- How would you define greatness?
- What would you like to be remembered for?
- If you were writing your own epitaph, what would it say?

No matter what questions you ask, it's extremely important that you listen carefully—and quietly—to the answers. Under no circumstances should you use the questions you ask or the answers you get as a platform from which to launch your own stories. That's a guaranteed way to demonstrate your sense of self-importance and lack of interest in the other person.

Funnel Questions

This technique involves starting with general questions, and then asking for more and more detail as you go along. It's often used by detectives who are taking a statement from a witness. It is a strategy for getting more deeply involved in a conversation with a person by finding out as much as you can. For example, my father used this method with any boy I had a date with in high school. It was miserable for me, but often my dad—in about 15 grueling minutes—knew more than I knew about the young man I was dating.

Funnel questions are good for finding out more detail about a specific point or person, and gaining the interest or increasing the confidence of the person with whom you're speaking. Asking "tell me more" questions will focus the other person on a particular area, thereby providing you with more information. And following those questions with precision words like "specifically," "actually," or "particularly" gives the person subtle direction to give you more detail in a particular area. Here's an example of how this might work: "You said that you began developing this product while you were in New York. What *specifically* prompted you to begin development of this product? When *exactly* did you begin?"

Don't Act as Smart as You May Be

Socrates used this technique more than 2,300 years ago, wherein he feigned ignorance in order to encourage others to express their views fully. Today, many of the world's smartest and fastest moving businesspeople have perfected the art—consciously or unconsciously—of disguising their intelligence. Socially intelligent people know that they always have something to learn, and if they ask lots of questions, they'll be better prepared to respond and then make a quick decision.

Downloadable Form 7.1: Self Assessment of "The Questions You Ask"

How well do you score on the following?

1. I ask good questions everyday.
   Always   Often   Sometimes   Never
2. I ask my spouse, significant other or children at least one open-ended question each day (just a personal test ☺).
   Always   Often   Sometimes   Never

3. I think through my questions before asking them.
Always   Often   Sometimes   Never

4. I do research before meeting with someone so I can ask the best questions.
Always   Often   Sometimes   Never

5. I know my best opening questions when I am first meeting someone.
Always   Often   Sometimes   Never

6. I ask questions of my colleagues everyday.
Always   Often   Sometimes   Never

7. I formally ask specific questions of my clients each year and record the answers to make the best decisions moving forward.
Always   Often   Sometimes   Never

8. I ask more questions when I think I'm dominating a conversation.
Always   Often   Sometimes   Never

9. I use Funnel Questioning Techniques when I want to find more facts.
Always   Often   Sometimes   Never

10. I ask questions even if I think I may know the answer.
Always   Often   Sometimes   Never

You can also access a free download of the self-assessment, "The Questions You Ask" at www.redzonemarketing.com/TheConnectors. Enter keycode "CONNECT" to download it for free!

In Other Words

A prudent question is one-half of wisdom.

Francis Bacon

Learn from others. Ask questions. Be a good listener. Get a pulse beat of what is going on around you.

Paul "Bear" Bryant

The art and science of asking questions is the source of all knowledge.
                                                    Thomas Berger

If you desire a wise answer, you must ask a reasonable question.
                                                    Johann von Goethe

The wise man doesn't give the right answers, he poses the right questions.
                                                    Claude Levi-Strauss

Take the attitude of a student, never be too big to ask questions, never know too much to learn something new.
                                                    Og Mandino

Successful people ask better questions, and as a result, they get better answers.
                                                    Tony Robbins

What I've learned is that people like to talk about themselves. And that's kind of the advantage you have when you're asking people questions.
                                                    Joe Sacco

No man really becomes a fool until he stops asking questions.
                                                    Charles P. Steinmetz

It is better to ask some of the questions than to know all the answers.
                                                    James Thurber

CHAPTER 8

Getting the Sale to Close Itself

Using Creative Strategies to Sell Without Selling

We have discussed ways that great connectors use to listen effectively and how they ask questions. However, you may be saying to yourself, "That's great, but how do you eventually get others to listen to *you*? Get them to act? To buy? To be an advocate? To become a client for life? If it's all about them, when does it become about *me*?"

When you make it about the other person, ask many questions, and curiously listen to the answer, you show others that you care, and by doing so you differentiate yourself. And that differentiation is the secret to eventually getting what you want in the most positive and natural way. Ultimately, the key in business is selling, and there is one main strategy for selling and selling more: closing! If, however, you concentrate all of your energy on *selling* something to someone, it no longer is all about what that other person wants or needs. It is now about what you want and need and that is not a positive closing strategy. Where the focus is placed is the key difference between selling and getting the sale to close itself.

In fact, if you started a relationship with a prospect by truly making it about their wants and needs, and then you turn the tables and try to sell them something, it breaks the connection that you've worked so hard to establish. If you lead the sale too much by using hard-line tactics, you may close the sale, but less often will there be the backend benefits to the sale that most great connectors enjoy. We have found that great connectors are able to close more sales and make it look easier in the process by utilizing and leveraging the work they've put into their relationships.

The sale closes itself because there is an overwhelming desire on the part of the buyer to *buy*. If someone wants what you have, wants to follow, wants to act, the sale simply closes itself.

Give 'em What They Want!

There is one fairly simple truth in the world of sales: If you have what buyers want, you don't *have* to sell. Wal-Mart founder Sam Walton said that his whole career was led by a single guiding principle: "The secret of successful retailing is to give your customers what they want." And instead of sitting in an office thinking about what they want, Walton was compelled to be with the employees and customers—on the front line—connecting with them. Even after he was diagnosed with fatal bone cancer, he spent his days flying his plane from town to town, going from Wal-Mart to Wal-Mart and visiting with his associates. Less than three weeks before Walton passed away, then-President George Bush flew to Bentonville, Arkansas, to present Walton with the Presidential Medal of Freedom. Instead of having a small event, Walton invited hundreds of his Wal-Mart associates to attend the ceremony. And the last person besides family he invited into his hospital room was a local Wal-Mart manager who discussed his store's sales figures for the week with Walton.

Over the years, Sam Walton not only gave his customers what they wanted (lowest possible prices, convenient hours, knowledgeable service, satisfaction guaranteed, and a friendly shopping experience), he gave his staff what they wanted too. In fact, he used his employees to spread his passion to the customers. Every Saturday morning, Walton would gather several hundred executives, managers, and associates at 7:30 AM to talk about business. They would start each of these meetings by doing the University of Arkansas's Razorback cheer. They also chanted their own Wal-Mart cheer. It may sound a bit corny, but these types of activities—along with Walton's personal style—created a company culture that made the associates feel differently about working there. It wasn't a job; it was more like a family.[1]

Three Strategies for Connecting and Closing Sales

The following strategies may seem like obvious ones in terms of closing sales, however, it is how they relate to relationships and connections that is significant. And the better we are at the connecting, the more sales we close and the easier we make it look in the process!

1. Creating the Feeling
2. Letting People Come to Their Own Conclusion
3. Cultivating Buyers

1. Creating the Feeling

Building the "I want that" situation for a prosective buyer is a simple key to closing more sales and closing them more easily. Most likely, no one would argue that. But it's not just a presentation of the features and benefits. It's more about how the prospective buyer believes the product will make them feel. If we can connect with a buyer emotionally, the sale will be quicker to close.

In 2000, Sara Blakely sold her first order of Spanx pantyhose to Neiman Marcus. By 2002, she was Ernst & Young's Entrepreneur of the Year award winner. And by 2008, Spanx had 75 employees, Sara personally had given away more than $1 million to charity, and her products had been featured in every major woman's magazine and on television shows like Oprah Winfrey, The Today Show, The View, Tyra Banks, and even networks like CNN. The story of her product appeared in magazines, newspapers, and news channels, and the garment itself was worn by countless celebrities.

But Blakely's success with Spanx was not due to her strong financial backing, a business school education (she had no formal business school education, and in fact, failed the law school admissions test—twice), or the many connections she possessed in the industry of women's undergarments. She had none of these things. Blakely was a sales trainer and stand-up comedian.

The first products Blakely sold were footless pantyhose that smoothed a woman's legs and buttocks. There are thousands of products available that claim to help women look better, shape their bodies, and perfect their look. So, why did Spanx take hold? Quite simply, Blakely was the connection to her product and was the catalyst in growing her firm. Instead of mailing samples to department stores requesting they buy her product, Blakely literally *showed* her Spanx. She personally called the buyer at Neiman Marcus and introduced herself over the phone. She told the buyer that she had invented a product their customers would not want to live without, and if she could have 10 minutes of the buyer's time, she would fly to Dallas. The buyer agreed.

Blakely said, "I had no shame . . . I asked her to follow me to the ladies room where I personally showed her the before/after in my cream pants. Three weeks later, SPANX was on the shelves of Neiman Marcus!" Blakely then called all her friends—including anyone she remembered just sitting next to in grade school—who lived in the cities where the product would be sold. She begged them to go to Neiman's and rave about the product and buy them up. Her current relationships—even the remote ones—were buying and creating buzz!

Blakely didn't tell; she showed. She revealed her own vulnerabilities, those that she knew many other women were likely to share, and personally displayed her product on her own body. And women began imagining how they would feel when they wore the undergarments.

Blakely knew that to take the product further, she would have to do some advertising to get the word out. But since she had no money to advertise, she hit the road. For the entire first year, Blakely personally did in-store rallies for Spanx with the sales associates, and then stayed all day introducing the store's customers to Spanx. She became notorious for lifting up her pant leg to every woman walking by. It wasn't just a product; it was, as Blakely showed, a way to make women look and feel more confident. And she invested of herself, her authenticity and her product. She connected, and the sales closed!

2. Letting Buyers Come to Their Own Conclusion

When we tell prospective buyers all about what we have to offer and why they should buy from us, we start onto a slippery slope that does not always end in a sale. Most buyers recognize the most obvious challenges and solutions that they have. They have most likely made conscious decisions using their best judgment to buy other products or services in the past. So if a salesperson begins even just by *inferring* that the prospect has made poor choices in the past— whether they have or not—the potential buyer will be less likely to listen. But if they are allowed to come to their own conclusion, the end result is much different.

There is a sales strategy called "The Wedge," originally defined by sales performance coach Randy Schwantz, which suggests that a salesperson should ask questions to which he may already know the answers.[2] Doing this may open up the buyer's eyes to other solutions without ever having to directly tell him about these options. In the case of Spanx, this is easy; I look in the mirror and realize this product will probably help me. But what if you are selling consulting services or some other less tangible and visible product? Consulting is not immediately emotional, and you can't see the results in the mirror as clearly or quickly.

So, for instance, I am meeting with a prospect who is interested in the services of my consulting firm. I am aware that there are many differences between my firm and the firm that the prospect is currently using. But if at any point during our meeting I tell my potential client the reasons why my firm is better, there is a high potential that he will get defensive. After all, he has made a conscious decision to use the other firm, and even if he isn't totally satisfied (that's why he's talking with me), I know that change is difficult and they don't want to necessarily admit a mistake in hiring the other firm. So instead of reciting a list of reasons why my firm is better, I may instead ask the prospective buyer a question like this:

> *"When your consulting firm meets with you monthly to go over your goal-to-actual marketing strategy results and a plan for modifications to impact sales, were you comfortable with that process?"*
>
> And your prospect says, *"Well . . . actually, we go over our goal-to-actual results only once a year, and we certainly haven't modified the plan monthly for improvements. Does your firm do that?"*

Presenting the features and benefits are not enough. Giving value-added ideas are not enough. The relationship itself is not enough. Most good salespeople do all of these things already. What great connectors do to close the sale is to research and ask the right questions, so the prospective buyer comes to his or her own conclusion that they must have whatever it is that you're selling. It's giving the buyer the ultimate respect and closing more sales at the same time— even when there is no competition against which you must compete.

3. Cultivating Buyers

Our Realtor is someone who successfully used the principles of "Getting the Sale to Close Itself." She, of course, received a commission when we completed the purchase of our new home. But there was absolutely no hard sell involved. She didn't have to spend a lot of time extolling the great features of the house, coming up with a long list of reasons why this was a great buy, pushing us into the sale, and telling us how foolish we'd be if we didn't gobble it right up. She found out what we really wanted in a house and what was important to us and then went out and found it. There wasn't much selling necessary.

Selling is about getting people to do something they haven't thought of already. Buying is taking into your possession what you have decided you want or need. You want buyers who don't need selling because they've already done it themselves. This is something renowned British tailor Richard Anderson has accomplished.

"Every time I see him, I buy something and feel great about it. But every time I saw him, I had NO intention of buying anything else. I have enough suits!" said a loyal customer of Richard Anderson, Ltd., a bespoke tailor located on Savile Row in London. This area of the city is world famous for its personalized tailoring excellence and tradition, where custom-made garments are completely original and unique to each customer.

Richard Anderson and his team make regular trips to service customers in the United States, Japan, and throughout Europe. They have some very famous clients, rock stars, bankers, lawyers, business executives, and even Simon Cowell from American Idol (yes, he wears suits). And they have an interesting model for selling custom-made suits to their thousands of repeat clients who spend on average $3,000 or more for a suit, sport coat, dinner jacket, or other completely custom-tailored item: They *never* sell.

Customers often schedule up to three fittings for one suit, and during those fittings the relationship is built. "Each time I go and see Richard Anderson, we end up chatting about each other's businesses—sometimes for 30 minutes or more after the fitting is complete. I feel like they really know *me*—not just my jacket size," a customer from the United States said. "When I meet with them, they show me a new fabric they have found—almost as an afterthought. They know I will like it, because they know me so well. I could shop for hours in a regular store and end up having the items I buy tailored anyhow. I may as well get something new and unique and get it done right the first time. Also, I have never been asked to buy a suit; they never had to."

Since 1982 when he was a 17-year-old apprentice, Richard Anderson has worked on Savile Row. He is master cutter, managing director, and co-founder of Richard Anderson Ltd., which opened in 2001 and is the youngest of these types of tailors on Savile Row. He is author of the book, *Bespoke: Savile Row Ripped and Smoothed*, published by Simon & Schuster Ltd., 2009. He has developed one of the most successful tailoring houses in the world through this personal service and a focus on the unique needs of his clients. And he has proven the theory that if you make a product that your customer truly wants to buy, you won't have to sell to them—even for a second.

The More Questions I Ask . . .

One of the most prolific connectors I have met in the financial services industry is located in Sarasota, Florida. He is without a doubt someone who has mastered the skills in the Red Zone Formula— and has enjoyed profitable results. When I first met him, I asked how he cultivated so many close relationships with extremely high-net-worth individuals who have invested with him. He told me, much to my surprise at the time, "It's because I'm a good listener." But as I came to find out, listening wasn't the only thing he did well. In the first meeting he has with a potential investor, he says that if he can simply ask questions for most of the meeting and talk minimally, the sale would just close itself.

His secret is the *way* he listens. It's the time and attention he expends, as well as the insightful questions he asks. It's the way that he avoids talking about himself, and his genuine attempt for total understanding of the prospect's situation. But more than any of these aspects individually, it is the totality of it all. He started using his complete questioning method after he switched firms and saw a lack in sales performance with prospects who didn't recognize the name of his new firm, a small independent investment company. He was very self-critical and assumed that he no longer understood why people bought or what caused them to purchase. So, out of desperation, he began asking lots of questions to figure out what was going on. And, the more questions he asked, the more he understood, and the longer he'd spend just listening, the more sales he began to close.

Getting to the Heart of the Matter

By asking these heart questions of his prospects, a Wisconsin-based financial advisor finds a way to relate to his prospects and close a high percentage of deals with everyone he meets (more than 90 percent). I asked this advisor what he credits for his incredibly high closing ratio. He thought about it and said, "Maribeth, my motto is, when she cries, she buys." I was immediately taken aback; I didn't think that this sounded like a relationship strategy at all. But then he explained.

In the process of discovering the key issues and financial concerns of a prospect, this advisor asks questions about something that is close to the heart of most people: their children or beneficiaries. He asks many questions about each child: how they handle money, where they went to college, and if they have children of their own. He asks questions about the children's character and finds out in a short period of time all about the family dynamics. Often times (and I have seen this firsthand myself while sitting in on a meeting with him), someone in the meeting becomes tearful when talking about their family. He says that if he gets to the heart of the issue, if he finds out what is truly important to the client, the sale no longer needs to be closed—it already is.

In fact, this advisor rarely talks about the financial products he sells. He uncovers what the client's most important issues are, talks generally about financial solutions, and then he leaves and asks his product specialist to come in to describe what they will be buying. He doesn't need to sell anything, because he says, "Once they get to an emotional state and have told me about things [that are] very important to them, the sale almost always closes." There was a trust from the beginning. And after they open up, they don't want to go anywhere else.

The Passionate Businessperson Is Always "Selling"

Often it is the passion of the businessperson that comes through so directly it pierces us and causes us to act. Are you delivering the passion that convinces others to buy or join you without you ever having to ask?

Downloadable Form 8.1: "Getting the Sale To Close Itself" Self Assessment

1. In sales meetings, I am listening and asking questions more than I am talking.
   Always   Often   Sometimes   Never

2. I never talk about the competition and compare myself.
   Always   Often   Sometimes   Never

3. I am giving people what they already want.
   Always   Often   Sometimes   Never

4. I do research before meeting with someone so I can ask "wedge" questions.
   Always   Often   Sometimes   Never

5. I ask "heart questions."
   Always   Often   Sometimes   Never

6. I show, not tell.
   Always   Often   Sometimes   Never

7. I create an emotional feeling during the sales process.
   Always   Often   Sometimes   Never

8. I use strategies other than hard selling tactics to close sales.
   Always   Often   Sometimes   Never

9. I really know my customers.
   Always   Often   Sometimes   Never

10. I let people come to their own conclusions.
    Always   Often   Sometimes   Never

You can also access a free download of the self-assessment, "Getting the Sale to Close Itself" at www.redzonemarketing.com/The Connectors. Enter keycode "CONNECT" to download it for free!

Create a Memorable Experience

Differentiating Yourself by the Impact You Leave on Others

T he final connector trait in the Red Zone Formula relates to the experience that is created for others. It is, ultimately, what you give.

The definition of an experience is something that engages people in a personal way unexpectedly. For instance, after going to a nice restaurant or a hotel, you say as you're leaving, "Wow! The food was incredible; the service was unbelievable; wow!" If, in fact, you actually *said* the word "wow," you most likely just have had an experience.

An experience isn't a large event or party. It is a gift of a connection that is made—either one-on-one or through a series of interactions. The overall feeling that is transferred is the experience. And the more memorable that feeling is, the more powerful the experience.

As your clients leave your place of business or hang up the phone, do they say "wow" about you? (In a good way, of course.)

A Hard Rock Experience

If you've ever been to one of the Hard Rock Hotels and you are a music lover, then the experience was likely quite memorable. As you enter the hotel, you realize it's not like any other that you've seen or stayed in. The music that is playing is bordering on loud, the lights are low enough that it's hard to see, and there are pictures and murals of rock stars covering all of the walls. When you check in, though, you probably don't even think that the process will be anything other than regular hotel business as usual. But upon doing so, you not only get a room key, but also a check-in CD that has all sorts of cool songs on it that you can play in the CD player in your room. Printed on the cover of the CD are lyrics from a popular song by the band Emerson, Lake and Palmer: "Welcome back my friends to the show that never ends, we're so glad you could attend, come inside, come inside." Then, in your room, you pick up the mini bar key and it says "Bottle of white, bottle of red" (from another popular song, this one by artist Billy Joel). As you make your way into the bathroom there is a placard that says, "I still haven't found what I'm looking for," from another well-known song by band U2. It tells you how you can access the Hard Rock's Forget Me Not Closet in case you've forgotten your toothbrush or your toothpaste or other necessity.

Now, in reality, this hotel's core offering is similar to other four-star hotels. The comfortable bed and plush pillows and maid service are all pretty much the same as in many other hotels. But the Hard Rock doesn't provide the same kind of hotel *experience*. And upon your departure from the Hard Rock, they hand you a checkout form with a quote from The Eagles song "Hotel California": "You can check out anytime you like, but you can never leave." From the moment you enter the Hard Rock until the moment you walk out, you are having a different kind of hotel experience. And it is a memorable one.

Give 'em Something to Talk about

To continue with our song lyrics-themed journey, in Bonnie Raitt's song "Something to Talk About," she sings that people are talking anyway, so let's *really* give them something to talk about. In business, however, people may not ever talk about you because nothing has struck them as unique or different. And of course, that's not good! Will clients want to remember the experience they had at your business? What is it that sets you apart from and above your competition? Have you given them something *good* to talk about? Oftentimes, it's the small surprises that truly get people talking. It would be a nice surprise if when you were checking out at a store the clerk took 10 percent off—just because. Or the manager came over and threw in something extra. That kind of behavior causes a connection and makes you feel good about that business, almost like you've made a new friend, and it leaves you with a memorable experience that is worth talking about. The experience is often the feeling that you've received something for nothing, a free gift of sorts. And, even to wealthier individuals, this gift creates feelings of achievement or winning.

It's All about the "Gift" You Give

One of my very favorite restaurants is Gramercy Tavern in New York City. It is consistently rated by Zagat® in the top 10 for all New York City restaurants, and is often even number one. I frequently share my experiences at Gramercy with friends, family, and business associates. I even talk about it in presentations I deliver to business audiences when defining an experience. But in describing the restaurant to others, I have realized that what I talk about are the unique differences—not the obvious things that may be expected.

Here is what the Gramercy Tavern has in common with other top-rated restaurants, which is probably why I don't talk about these attributes:

1. The food is exceptional: as it is at most New York City restaurants that are highly rated by Zagat® at a similar price point.

2. The chef designs a menu like an artist using ingredients that reflect the particular time of year, and there are always updated and seasonal items. This is what restaurants often do and is not incredibly unique for a fine-dining restaurant.

3. It is a popular place. You need a reservation to get in, because it seems everyone in New York City wants to eat here and have thought—sometimes even a month in advance— to reserve a table: Most great New York City restaurants don't ever have open tables and require reservations.

These are all givens; they are not particularly unique or exciting, especially for New York. They are all the attributes that we come to expect from these type of restaurants. However, here's what is different about Gramercy Tavern and what I often find myself talking about:

1. The wait staff is *beyond* attentive, but in a highly trained, non-obtrusive way. They seem to never interrupt a conversation and never, ever make you feel rushed to leave. I've been there before for as long as three hours, just eating and talking! And while there may be as many as five or six people who are attending to the various needs at the table, you barely notice most of them. If you need something, merely lifting your head from the conversation usually prompts your main waiter to come over. If you want a live example of great service, this place is it!

2. The restaurant is so alive and bristling with energy. You feel different when you are in there, as though you are in a special place that others love too. There is conversation, laughing, and people everywhere, but you can clearly have a private conversation with the people at your table without straining. I've seen David Letterman and other celebrities dining at Gramercy; it is an exciting place to be.

3. When you are done with your meal, have paid, and are getting up to leave, someone from the wait staff comes over to hand you a gift—a cranberry orange muffin wrapped in cellophane with long ribbons tying if off. "For your breakfast tomorrow morning," the waiter says. And of all the things that they do at Gramercy Tavern, this is the number one thing I tell others about. Because it's something that you receive after all of the expected has been delivered. A gift for *me*? The first time I really thought it was a one-time thing; something just for me, the new customer (naïve, I know). But it happens every time. And, I always eat the muffin the next morning for breakfast and think about my evening at Gramercy Tavern. Gramercy is not in the muffin business; they are in the experience business.

Gramercy Tavern is part of The Union Square Hospitality Group, which was founded by restauranteur Danny Meyer and includes 11 highly acclaimed, distinctive restaurants in the New York City area. To maintain the high quality of food and service consistently is more than a grand challenge in the restaurant business. So how have they consistently beaten the odds? After reading Meyer's book, *Setting the Table: The Transforming Power of Hospitality in Business* (Harper Collins 2006), it is clear that delivering an experience is actually his focus. His mantra in the restaurant business is to deliver what he calls "enlightened hospitality." This philosophy emphasizes putting the power of hospitality to work in a new and counterintuitive way: The first and most important application of customer service is to the people who work for you, and then, in descending order of priority, to the guests, the community, the suppliers, and the investors. This way of prioritizing is not traditional in the restaurant business or many others, but Meyer considers it the foundation of every success that he and his restaurants have achieved. The fact is that whatever business you are in, whatever skills you have, whatever industry in which you excel, don't assume that what people are talking about is actually the core of what you do or provide. People are looking for something worth talking about, the unexpected. What are the unexpected offerings you have that people could or should be talking about?

The Unexpected Attributes of Your Business That People Could Talk About:

1. _____
2. _____
3. _____
4. _____
5. _____

Energy Exchange Creates the Experience

It has been said that up to 85 percent of your success and happiness will come from your relationships and interactions with others. The more positively others respond to you, the easier it will be for you to get the things you want. That is the natural byproduct of the experience you create for others. If you were told that you were going to meet a very wealthy entrepreneur who was very quiet and unassuming about her success, you may assume that this person is filled with charisma. And you may not act the same in her presence if you had been told nothing at all. The most important thing about charisma is that it is largely based on *perception*, on the conclusions that people have already made or would like to believe. For example, perceived charisma can be created in another person by speaking in very positive terms about that person to a third party. And, if you believe that you are about to meet an outstanding and important person, that person will tend to have charisma for you.

So, charisma—for the most part—begins largely in the mind of the beholder. But the energy you give to others is not perception. In a sense, you are a living magnet, and you are constantly releasing and attracting energy waves. This energy is intensified by passion.

And if you are incredibly passionate about something, other people assume it must be something worth being passionate about, and they will begin to sense that.

I have often heard people refer to someone as having a "magnetic personality." From what I have observed in successful businesspeople, this magnetism is real, however, the place from which it originates is the key. It is what you do for others that attract them to you. If you have power, money, or celebrity, you are providing other people with access to something that they don't have. But more important, magnetism is caused by how you make others feel.

Many very successful businesspeople release a great deal of energy and, in essence, give it to others. In our pursuit of significance, we unleash energy and passion. Energy and passion cause inspiration to others, and it comes in different ways. They may buy from you, they may follow you, or they may talk about you. But only an inspired person can deliver energy and passion and truly make a difference in others around them.

Customercentric

A memorable experience is one that delights customers. Think about your own purchasing behavior. When was the last time you were truly *delighted* by a business transaction? Why? Chances are, if you are delighted about a buying experience you had, it may have been the process as much as the product that made you feel that way. And when we are excited, we tend to talk about it to anyone who will listen. We talk or create buzz when a salesperson goes out of his or her way to simplify our life; when we received more for our money than we expected; when we were treated like the company's most important customer; when we feel smart, fulfilled, or excited about a purchase we made; or when we experience something new or extraordinary.

In working with large and small businesses, we have observed that the experiences these firms create are often manifested during the specific development of delighted clients. Clients want to be pleased, and we want them to feel that way. Many companies focus primarily on their revenues, profitability, operational efficiency, organizational structure, product or service development, and pricing strategies. But companies are finding more success by also thinking externally in customercentric ways. And recent research from Accenture confirms it.

Insights from the 2008 Accenture Customer Satisfaction Survey underscore the critical importance of delivering a customer-centric service experience in the current global economy. Based on the responses of 4,189 consumers surveyed in Australia, Brazil, Canada, China, France, Germany, India, the United Kingdom and the United States, an outward focus on the customer appears more essential than ever to acquiring and retaining profitable customer relationships. According to this Accenture study, how well companies understand and meet the distinct preferences and expectations of the customers they serve had a powerful influence over those customers' willingness to remain versus their propensity to leave.

The analysis says that "In fact, consumers participating in the study ranked the quality of the customer experience as the primary reason why they chose to leave providers during the past year—cited even more often than finding a better price somewhere else, despite the economic uncertainty faced by consumers in many of these markets." We are clearly in an era where "delighting" customers is critical, maybe more than ever. Research from Cap Gemini Ernst and Young back this up: "Consumers don't differentiate retailers by their value propositions." It's what they actually deliver.

But Do People Want *Your* Experience?

In the early '90s, I worked for the Washington Bullets (now called the Washington Wizards) NBA basketball team, and at that time there were 40 people in the sales staff charged with selling tickets. We didn't have the top-name players in the NBA at the time, and we had to work hard to sell Bullets tickets. At the same time, in the middle of the country, there was probably just one guy sitting behind a desk telling callers, "Sorry, we're sold out." People had already lined up around the block to buy tickets to the Michael Jordan, Chicago Bulls' experience.

I often ask businesses this question: Are you selling, or do people want what you have? If you create a memorable experience, people will line up to do business with you. But it's not just good service that is noted or remembered these days. In fact, people *expect* quality service; that in and of itself cannot be the entire experience for them. Businesspeople will often say to me that they don't understand why they don't get more referrals. Their clients are pleased, the service is always top-notch, and they're giving the customers what they want. But, that's it! If you simply give them what they want, it isn't an experience. They have to *want* what you have!

The Cheesehead Phenomenon

A sign of an experience takes place when you find yourself doing things you wouldn't usually do. I'm a Green Bay Packer fan, born and raised in Wisconsin. You may have noticed that many Packer fans wear on their heads what is commonly referred to as a "cheesehead." Now, really, what would possess someone of seemingly normal intelligence to wear a cheesehead? And in public? And want to be on TV in front of millions of people?

The Cheesehead Phenomenon occurs when the experience causes us to do something we wouldn't otherwise do. It is like, for instance, when your clients go out of their way to help you, send business your way, or drop you a note of thanks—something they otherwise ordinarily would not do. Most people are thinking about themselves and their own lives. If we can get them to think about us for a little bit, we must have created a memorable experience.

The Packer experience comes from generations of adoring fans who have backed this team through many years of losing in the same way they have supported them through many years of winning. Loyal fans do just that. Packer fans have a great desire to be a part of the experience of going to a game at Lambeau Field. They outwardly share their pride for their team and the State of Wisconsin, starting with a non-negotiable necessity of creating or attending a pre-game tailgate party filled with lots of brats, beer, and cheese. Fans wear all sorts of cheesehead gear and other unique hunting clothing (the warmest clothing you can get for the Northwoods fans). People are there for the game, to see their beloved team win, and for the fun. But they would show up *without* the game (they do this for any event related to the team). They show up when the team has a losing record. They come merely for the connection with like-minded people and the thrill of the thought of winning. Attending a game at Lambeau Field is truly an experience.

Individuals Create a Brand Experience

Just like the Green Bay Packers, for any brand to remain relevant, there is a need for an emotional attachment to that brand. But many businesspeople do not look at themselves as a "brand." I don't mean that we should think immediately about putting our faces on a billboard or some other large-scale advertising and branding campaign. But those who connect at a higher level have created a memorable brand, of sorts. They leave something behind with the people they touch—a memory, a thought, a connection. And some of the best connectors take absolute control over their personal brands. If they did not, others would and could define them. For your personal brand to be successful or memorable, a deliberate effort may be necessary to create true experiences for those around you.

I know of a Realtor® in an area of the country very active with listings who has hundreds of competitors with access to the same inventory and whose fees are identical to his. Nevertheless, he's the first Realtor® most people in the area call when they're ready to put their homes on the market.

Why? Sure, he puts up signs, runs ads, holds open houses, and shows properties—just like every other Realtor® does. But that's not what sets him apart. Unlike his competitors, he doesn't just show up when someone wants to buy or sell a house. Each spring, every homeowner in the area gets a tiny tree from him to replant in his or her yard, and in October, a pumpkin with a note from him appears on each front porch. In mid-summer, his antique fire engine, loaded with neighborhood kids, is at the head of the local Independence Day parade.

His investment in his exposure and his brand is one that pays rich dividends year after year. He's become the top Realtor® in his area because he does what his competitors don't do—he creates experiences!

The Age of Experience

It's really a whole new world out there. What was once the Agrarian Age (200 years ago) gave way to the Industrial Age, which then evolved into the Information Age. Today, according to authors B. Joseph Pine II and James H. Gilmore, the Information Age has been replaced by the Experience Age.

In their book, *The Experience Economy: Work Is Theatre & Every Business a Stage* (Harvard Business School Press, 1999), Pine and Gilmore issue a warning: "Those businesses that relegate themselves to the diminishing world of goods and services will be rendered irrelevant. To avoid this fate, you must learn to stage a rich, compelling experience."

Therefore, the way to really rise above the competition, delight your customers, receive stellar ratings, and protect your client base is to create an experience for them. You don't want to be or become a commodity; even service-based businesses today are becoming "commoditized." A commodity is something that's capable of being interchanged or replaced. They can't be differentiated from one another, and their prices are solely determined by market demand.

What is the differentiation you have? It's probably *you*! And, that's where the real experience comes in. We have the ability to change the way someone feels and create a memorable experience that keeps clients coming back for more. Think of some memorable experiences you've enjoyed. These experiences—like the ones you receive at a theme park, a unique restaurant, or event—are planned. The companies involved carefully design the experience they want their clients to have.

Consider bookstores, for example. Once upon a time, about all they included were rows of bookshelves and a cash register. You went in, found the books you wanted, paid your bill, and left. They were basically in the commodity business. Not anymore! Today's typical bookstore features comfortable furniture where you can sit and read to your heart's content. You'll also find a wide array of magazines, local and out-of-town newspapers, perhaps even a section where you can buy or trade used books, and of course, a refreshment area where you can enjoy an almost limitless variety of coffee products or soft drinks, bagels, doughnuts, sandwiches, and cookies. Bookstores have actually become a place to socialize.

On a recent visit to one of the large chain bookstores, I found nearly all of the above—plus gifts, greeting cards, puzzles, games, stationery, calendars, music CDs, fine chocolates, and more. And for the shoppers who actually wanted to look at some books but had left their glasses at home, the store also sold—you guessed it—reading glasses!

While there, I was given a copy of the store newsletter and an application to join its frequent-buyer club. One store official told me the chain does $15 million a year in sales—of chocolates! And it sells more coffee to its customers than all but the largest coffee outlets. Everything in the store says, "Come in and stay for a while; relax and enjoy your visit." It's no longer a matter of simply buying a book or two. It's been transformed into an experience!

How Are You Creating the Experience?

Think creatively about how you personally create an experience. For example, I have one client who is very health conscious. He wants everyone around him to live healthier, more active lives. So he incorporates healthy food, videos, books, posters, and seminars into his unrelated business offerings. He's providing an experience—a total healthy life plan that focuses on his clients' overall well-being and connecting with people on a different level.

Another long-time client of mine provides postcards featuring photos of his office to his valued clients as they're finishing up their appointments. The clients address the cards to their friends and associates, and my client stamps and mails them. It's akin to going on vacation; you want to share the experience with your friends, so you send a postcard. You could also print buttons or T-shirts with the name of your business and the experience on it.

Another client has created "The Life Enjoyment Experience®," the idea being that he helps his clients "get to the top of the mountain." From the mountaintop, you can see and experience the enjoyment of the world. Therefore, he has decorated each office and conference room in his headquarters to represent a different part of the world. One room has a huge mural of London on the wall; another one represents Washington, DC. He reports that people bring their friends by to see his unique facilities, even without an appointment. Can you imagine a better way to attract new business?

That's one of the great things about experiences: People who have positive ones want to share them with others. Bear in mind as well that clients will pay a premium for an experience—meaning you'll receive greater revenue per client, you'll increase your client retention, and you'll acquire more clients at a lower cost.

It's More Than the Product You Sell

Is it the best burger in the world? Or is it something else that keeps us buying?

Born in Atlantic City, New Jersey, in 1932, he never knew his birth parents, but was adopted and raised by a couple from Lebanon. He got his first job at age 12, was fired not long afterward, and then dropped out of high school at age 15 to work as a busboy at a restaurant. After the Korean War broke out in 1950, he enlisted in the U.S. Army. Honorably discharged in 1953, he took a job at a Kentucky Fried Chicken restaurant.

He was 21 years old, and there was little—if anything—in his life up to that point that gave a hint of future success or greatness. But once granted the opportunity to work directly with KFC founder Colonel Harland Sanders, he became inspired, performed well, and before long, owned several KFC franchises. Yet he'd had a dream, since childhood, of owning a hamburger restaurant, so he later sold his KFC stores to pursue that dream.

In 1969, this 37-year-old high school dropout opened his first restaurant in Columbus, Ohio, naming it after his eight-year-old daughter, whose nickname was—you guessed it—Wendy! The rest, of course, is history.

Dave Thomas appeared in the hamburger company's advertisements for 13 years. The long-running Dave Thomas Campaign made him one of the nation's most recognizable spokespeople. Americans loved him for his down-to-earth, sometimes goofy, wholesome style. He connected with people because he didn't stand apart from the average person. "From the very beginning, I never thought of myself as anybody special. And whatever I've accomplished throughout my life, when I look in the mirror, I still see myself as a hamburger cook," Thomas said.

Thomas connected with his customers—even through the TV. And they remembered him and his restaurant, and they kept going back. There have been many other spokespeople at many companies, but few created the connection with people like Thomas did. He was the one creating the experience and convincing people they wanted what his restaurant had.

Being Authentic

We often connect with people for one simple reason: They seem similar to us. They are not above us or condescending. They have gone through tough times, they are not perfect, they face the same issues and problems that we do, and that's attractive. The underdog who has made it still looks and sounds the same; we love it, and we connect with this person. The connection is emotional on some level, and it causes us to do things that we wouldn't have without the feeling.

Still Creating the Experience Today

Though business experts may point to different elements of Wendy's operations as the reason for its success, to Dave it all came down to one thing: the customers. "If we take care of our customers every day and exceed their expectations, we'll earn their loyalty and they will keep coming back," he said. And they did.

But the Dave Thomas story is about more, much more, than just building the third-largest chain of fast-food restaurants in the world. With all the success he enjoyed, he never lost sight of the fact that he'd been adopted, and he was determined to come to the aid of other children who needed someone to love and care for them.

Thomas died of cancer in 2002, but his foundation's work goes on. Each year, it conducts National Adoption Day, and on that day in the year 2008 alone, more than 4,000 children were formally adopted. Even years after his death, Dave Thomas continues to create an indelible footprint on the lives of the countless thousands of children being raised by loving parents who chose them. They are a living testimony to the way he still creates an experience for others.

What "Gifts" Are You Giving to Others?

If we concentrate on creating a memorable impact upon the people we touch, an authentic presentation of ourselves and our company, there is no doubt that connections will come easier, referrals will come faster, and a stream of business will come in.

So give yourself the following analysis. How well are you doing in creating experiences for others?

Downloadable Form 9.1: "Unique Elements of the Business"

List 5 unique elements of what you do. Will people talk about them?

1. _____
2. _____
3. _____
4. _____
5. _____

You can also access a free download of the worksheet, "Unique Elements of the Business" at www.redzonemarketing .com/TheConnectors. Enter keycode "CONNECT" to download it for free!

The True Litmus Test—Ask Others!

Create an advisory board comprised of clients, associates, and employees to give you feedback on the experience that you are creating. Invite these people to join you for an evening, and ask them to help you look forward in your business. Some common advisory board questions that will stimulate valuable discussions on the experiences you are providing are:

1. "Why did you choose to do business with this firm?"
2. "Why will you stay with this firm?"
3. "Why would you introduce others to this firm?"
4. "What are you looking for from this firm?"

5. "What would delight you?" (a question to garner more detail on this: "Have you ever been delighted by another business; how did they do it?")

6. "What is your perception of this industry?"

7. "Why would someone else hire a firm like ours?"

8. "Why *wouldn't* someone hire our firm?"

9. "Where do you believe we should look for additional target clients that our firm is built to service?"

10. "Are there other target markets upon which we should be focusing?"

11. "Are there marketing activities that we should be using to attract target clients?"

12. "What do you think of our review process? How could we improve it?"

13. "What do you like/not like about our office space?"

14. "How could we improve your service overall?"

15. "What is your opinion and feedback on the quality of our office staff?"

16. "What are educational topics and/or events that you would find valuable?"

17. "Do you like our client appreciation events? How could we make them better?"

18. Other _____

For a complete outline of how to organize an effective advisory board meeting, please go to www.redzonemarketing.com/The Connectors. Enter keycode "CONNECT" to download it for free!

Applying the 5 Connector Traits

Gain a Stream of Profitable Referrals

The Litmus Test for Relationship Success

I f you provide valuable, worthwhile products and services to your clients, then they'll want to share you with others. It's just human nature! But how consistently do you receive referrals? When we look at what successful businesspeople do to receive high-quality referrals consistently, it is all about the development of the relationship.

However, in the acquisition of referrals, many businesspeople have focused on asking for referrals as their main strategy for receiving them. And, although asking for referrals does work, what we have observed is that more often than not it is a frustrating way of attempting to get referrals. It's not because you're not referable. There may be a disconnect between you and your client that is affecting the number of referrals you receive, no matter how often you ask for them.

The Worst-Case Scenario

We will, for better or worse, consider the worst-case scenario that we'd like to avoid before taking action. In contemplating whether to refer a friend, colleague, or family member to another professional, we may consciously or subconsciously consider the potential things that could go wrong. Will it work out? Will it make me look bad? Will something go wrong? If there is even the slightest inkling that this might not go well, the referrals will not come.

The Reasons We May Not Get the Referrals We Deserve

Most businesspeople would probably agree that they would like to get more referrals or recommendations and have more raving fans. The critical question that you must ask yourself when considering why you might not be receiving more of these are:

A. *Have you taken the time to develop a relationship?*
B. *Do people have something unique to say to others about you?*
C. *Are you truly referable or could you be more referable?*

Let's look at each question individually.

A. Have You Taken the Time to Develop a Relationship?

Dr. Ivan Misner, founder and chairman of BNI, the world's largest business networking and referral organization, has written a total of 11 books, including his #1 bestseller, *Business by Referral*, and his New York Times bestseller, *Truth or Delusion*. Misner has established what he calls the VCP® Process of building relationships and acquiring referrals. It is an eye-opening and insightful method that provides the blueprint for *successful* referral acquisition.

The VCP® PROCESS (As described in *Business by Referral*, Bard Press Inc., 1998):

PHASE 1- Visibility: The first phase of growing a relationship takes place when you and another individual become aware of each other. This phase creates recognition and awareness. The greater your visibility, the more widely known you will be, the more opportunities you will be exposed to, and the greater your chance of being accepted by others as someone to whom they can—or should—refer business. Visibility must be actively maintained and developed; without it you cannot move on to the next level: credibility.

PHASE 2- Credibility: Once you and your new acquaintance form expectations of one another—and once these expectations begin to be fulfilled—your relationship can enter the credibility stage. Credibility grows when expectations are met. Referrals won't come unless your counterpart knows who you are (visibility) and considers you a credible businessperson.

PHASE 3- Profitability: A mature relationship is one that is defined as being profitable, in which both partners gain satisfaction. If a connection doesn't benefit both partners, it probably will not endure. Profitability in a referral relationship is not found by bargain hunting; it must be cultivated, and this takes patience.

"[It is] a chronological process," Misner said. "You must first be visible—who you are and what you do. Then, you have to establish credibility—are you good at it? That takes time to develop. Only after these 2 steps are fulfilled will the other person be willing to have a reciprocal relationship based on the exchange of referrals." And rushing the process does not work with consistency. "Even if someone comes highly recommended," Misner said, "they will still need to confirm it themselves."

Establishing visibility and credibility are the steps in the process where the relationship is built. So it is no wonder that those who

try to speed up the process by handing you a business card at a networking event and suggest you do business with them rarely produce results. There is no relationship, yet.

Take Action to Build Client Relationships

smith&jones is a marketing and advertising firm located in Stur-
bridge, MA, with clients from all across the United States. The
co-owners, Christine Tieri and Jean Giguere, admit that when
they set out in business they certainly didn't intend to set up
relationships with the idea that they would last longer than the
job at hand. They concentrated on launching the business, getting the jobs out the door, and not looking much further down
the road than their next sale. "With all the statistics of new businesses not making it past the one- or five-year mark, you are not
really concentrating on building relationships for life, but luckily
for us (13 years later), along the way—we did," says Tieri, the
firm's creative director. "Two of our largest clients at the agency
today are also our oldest clients—and that is unheard of in the
ad business where often clients change agencies as often as fash-
ion trends. And many of our other clients have also been with us
for numerous years."

In building their multimillion dollar firm, Tieri and Giguere realized that although they didn't make a deliberate effort, their firm
has been built on maintaining and cultivating relationships. It's
simply how they do business, and the almost unintended results
have been referrals from their clients. However, if they spent time
asking for referrals as a strategy, that would never have produced
the advocates and referrals that they enjoy today. The acquisition
of referrals relies on a process and a business philosophy.

"We have always felt strongly about giving back to our community. We've had one pro-bono client for over eight years. This organization hasn't paid us one cent while we have provided tens of
thousands of dollars in marketing," said Giguere, the firm's account
director. "But, the director is so well-loved in the community—and

he sings our praises louder than anyone we know—that we have received so many excellent referrals from him. Therefore, our relationship with this organization has paid dividends and potential clients love us for just being associated with this organization and its dynamic director."

Here are some of Tieri and Giguere's common sense and quite successful keys to maintaining relationships resulting in referrals and a steady stream of business. They make good business sense, of course, but it's the philosophy that produces so much more!

smith&jones Business Mantra

1. View Each Business Relationship Like a Friendship: We try to do business with people we like and trust, and whose work ethic and philosophies we appreciate. We realize that our clients and vendors feel the same, so we view each new business relationship like you would a friendship—one where we seek common ground based on mutual respect.

2. Share Objectives with Your Clients: When business objectives are the same, we find that our business relationships run deep. Common goals are more easily met by working together, and long-lasting relationships are forged because of the mutual objectives that we share with our clients.

3. Develop a Partnership with Clients: We never think of our relationships with clients as "us and them." We truly feel we are partners with our clients, and delve into their businesses as if they were our own. We take on their challenges, we immerse ourselves in their industries, and we come to understand their needs. When we do this, our clients sense that we feel their pain and that we stand with them in achieving their goals.

4. Take it Personally: Every day we are faced with decisions, most with ethical ramifications. It could be about containing costs, managing expectations, dealing with an error, or

handling disagreements. We don't separate the way we act in our personal lives with how we act at work. We've learned that the world is small, paths will cross again, and taking the high road is always the best decision.

5. Lend a Helping Hand: We've had a few colleagues over the years who have been between jobs—either exploring consulting or starting their own business—and we have helped them with logos or small brochures and web sites. We do this because we are appreciative of the work they have given us in the past and value our relationship—not for any promise of work in the future. However, almost every single time the colleague has moved on to better, more wonderful jobs or their start-up has blossomed, they have rewarded our agency with their new business.

6. Take Part in the Community: Over the years, we have served on area boards, including an advertising club, an educational foundation, a civic improvement group, and a chamber of commerce. By participating in area organizations and joining our colleagues in improving our area, we show our commitment to a longer-term presence in our community.

7. Give Back: While we are a for-profit business, we do our share of pro-bono work for nonprofit clients. In fact, we participate in CreateAthon (http://www.smithnjones.com/create.htm), which is an annual 24-hour creative blitz where we donate work for multiple, local nonprofit clients. We don't do this in hopes that we will get good PR, or that these nonprofits will miraculously come up with money to hire us. We do it because we believe in their causes, and because it's one way that we can use our talents and resources to give back to our community. And in doing so, we have met fabulously wonderful people who have not only brought us macaroni and cheese at midnight to keep us going, but also are people who we enjoy meeting up with again and again at community events and admire the blood, sweat, and tears they put into their organizations every day.

B. Do People Have Something Unique to Talk About?

In Misner's years of experience working and studying successful professionals, he has determined that "success is the uncommon application of common knowledge."

The uncommon application is the differentiator, the attractor of the connection, and the key factor in success. It goes beyond passion, drive, hard work, intelligence, and making good decisions (typically thought of as some main success factors). And it is what gets people talking about you and your company.

"Achieving success in business is simple, but not easy," Misner said. "If it were easy, then everyone would be successful. But it is so simple that people often look elsewhere for more complex ways."

The truth is that if you perform up to the minimum expectations of the client—in other words, you give them exactly what they feel they are paying you for and nothing more—then there is not much to talk about. There is no experience. But if you exceed their expectations, they will have something unique to share. And rarely are our expectations exceeded in business anymore.

Communicating with Your Clients

A financial advisor in the Midwest had a great eye-opener in regards to the simple acquisition of referrals. During his first eight years in business, he had accumulated $10 million of investment assets that he managed for his clients. He was acquiring 80 percent of his new clients by prospect marketing—seminars, direct mail, networking, and phone calling—and 20 percent by referrals from his current clients.

In his ninth year in business, he decided to begin communicating more consistently with his current clients. He implemented a series of actions to regularly reach out to his current clients with the same intensity and purpose as he did with prospecting for new clients.

The client marketing system he used included the following strategies:

- Regular phone and mail communication to his clients
- Client-focused educational seminars and events
- Open houses
- Commitment to periodic client reviews
- Ongoing client-appreciation activities, including notes, letters, cards, gifts, and social events.

During the three years following the implementation of this client communication/marketing plan, his business increased from $10 million to $100 million in investments that he managed for clients. A significant and surprising jump in just three years! And it didn't end there. By the end of the fifth year, he had $200 million under management. His secret was adding client marketing to the mix. The result was a significant upsurge in well-qualified, easy-to-close referrals from his current clients.

In his book *Getting Clients, Keeping Clients*, Dan Richards describes another example of how well client marketing works using a case called the Rule of 11. In this instance, he took an office of 12 financial advisors who wanted to build their businesses. Six of them concentrated solely on seminars, advertising, cold calling, and networking to generate business. In other words, they focused on "cold" prospecting. The other six concentrated solely on client workshops and newsletters, and on an overall heightened contact level with clients. In other words, they focused on *client* marketing. The result was that the group that concentrated on current clients proved 11 times more effective than the six who marketed only to prospects. Imagine 11 times more in sales revenues achieved simply by cultivating the relationships you already have.

Delighted Clients Become Evangelists for You!

When customers are truly delighted about their experience with your product or service, they can become outspoken advocates for your company. This group of satisfied believers can be your most powerful marketing force to gain sales and increase your exposure and influence.

In their book *Creating Customer Evangelists*, authors Ben McConnell and Jackie Huba profile highly successful companies to illustrate the power that solid customer relationships build. They explain how organizations such as Southwest Airlines, the Dallas Mavericks, IBM, and others effectively built their customer base and created targeted marketing programs to involve their biggest fans. These programs have produced an entire force of unofficial salespeople.

By deepening customer relationships, profitable organizations create communities that generate grassroots support and value for their products and services. *Creating Customer Evangelists* focuses on this ultimate marketing approach, as the authors demonstrate how you can convert good customers into exceptional ones who willingly spread the word about your business.

From their research into the best practices of some of the most forward-thinking companies with legions of evangelists who spread the word, McConnell and Huba outline and explain the six basic tenets of creating customer evangelists:

1. Continuously gather customer feedback.
2. Make it a point to share knowledge freely.
3. Build word-of-mouth networks.
4. Create community: Encourage communities of customers to meet and share.
5. Create bite-size chunks: Devise specialized, smaller offerings to get customers to bite.
6. Create a cause: Focus on making the world, or your industry, better.

Dropping the Ball on Business and Referrals

Delighted clients are loyal and will stay with you—sometimes forever. Dissatisfied clients not only go elsewhere, but they also tell others of their dissatisfaction. And, in most cases, they won't even tell you they're dissatisfied. In fact, for each one who does complain to you, there are on average nine others who'll just disappear without bothering to tell you why.

What's even worse is that those dissatisfied clients will each tell an average of five other people about their displeasure with you. That means that for every complaint, you could have up to 60 people who are walking around with a negative image of you and your company—and are talking about it! I call it "The Rule of 60."

It is actually scary how much damage even one displeased client can cause you in your pursuit of good word-of-mouth referrals. For example, a colleague of mine took some important clients to dinner at an expensive out-of-town restaurant where they unfortunately experienced both terrible food and terrible service. To top it off, they had barely finished their meal when the manager asked if they'd mind moving to the bar, as others were waiting for their table.

My colleague expressed his outrage in a long letter to the restaurant owner, who called him—three months later—to apologize and plead for a second chance, inviting him to bring his wife to dinner "on the house." He did so and, after the meal, was given a bill. When he mentioned the owner's offer, he was told that it covered the meal only and that he was responsible for paying for the appetizers, beverages, and dessert.

Now, here's the rest of the story in my colleague's own words: "Ironically, about a year later, we moved much closer to that town, and as I passed that restaurant every day on my way to and from work, I thought about the awful experiences we had there. Neighbors often asked if I knew anything about that particular restaurant, and I probably told my story more than 75 or even 100 times. Each time I did, the reaction was the same: 'Oh, thanks for telling us what happened to you. We almost made a huge mistake.'"

Perhaps so, but it wouldn't have been nearly as large a mistake as that restaurant owner made. Presented with the opportunity to make amends for bad service and to salvage a customer, she instead made things much worse—all for a measly few dollars. In the long run, it probably cost her far more than she could even begin to calculate.

Incidentally, that particular colleague also happened to be an executive with a 2,500-member business association and often used that story during customer-service workshops—identifying the restaurant by name!

A study by the American Society for Quality Control on why companies lose customers warned: "Unless a customer is completely satisfied—to the point of being positively delighted and willing to brag about the product or service received—there exists great potential for market damage and future trouble for the company."

The Lifetime Value of a Client

Estimating the lifetime value of a client can be a real eye-opener. For instance, a Taco Bell customer isn't merely someone who walks in today and spends three or four dollars for lunch. Taco Bell has estimated that the lifetime value of that customer is an amazing $12,000. That's a whole lot of burritos, amigo! For automobile manufacturers, the lifetime value of a customer averages $340,000.

But, when you add the referrals your loyal clients give you and the revenue they have generated, the numbers can get very large—very quickly.

A colleague who produces newsletters for various business clients never views any of them as merely the source of $1,000 income for him this month. He knows from experience that each of those clients, over the long term, represents significant revenue for him, and he treats each accordingly. One client used his services for 12 years, generating nearly $200,000 in income for him.

To calculate the lifetime value of your clients, here are the factors you should know. You can use a client-rating formula based on revenue generated, referrals, future potential, influence, time spent servicing, and other factors, both quantitative and qualitative. The reason you want to take the time to go through this rating exercise is so that you can concentrate your marketing efforts on the clients who mean the most to your business and those prospects who fit that same profile.

C. Are You Truly Referable—or Could You Be More Referable?

Good businesspeople are referable, for the most part. If you were to ask all of your current clients if they would ever refer business to you, most would say that they would. In fact, for healthy businesses, 80 percent of the clients on average would say that they would give you a referral. So, why don't they?

The first question you ask yourself is "Am I referable?" And the answer is often, "yes." But if you believe you are delighting your clients and still not receiving regular referrals from them, it's possible that there may be a disconnect. The insider perception of the business is not the same as how the clients of the business actually see things. And while it doesn't mean that you must be doing something wrong, it's worth checking out.

One way to find out for sure is to conduct a "Client Delight Survey." You can mail or email the survey, or you can use an online survey service like www.surveymonkey.com to give your clients an easy way to provide you with feedback. You can easily design your survey online and send a link to your clients for access. You can then view your results as they are collected in real-time, including live graphs and charts and then see individual responses. There are also functions that allow you to download a summary of your results and even download all the raw data and export it to a spreadsheet for further analysis.

Some typical survey questions are (graded A-F):

1. Our organization is totally committed to the idea of keeping you informed and satisfied. _____

2. Rather than having to undo mistakes, we seem to "do things right the first time." _____

3. Our organization appears to be totally committed to the idea of quality. _____

4. We regularly provide information of value to you. _____

5. We have adequate contact with you. _____

6. We make it easy for you to do business with us. _____

7. Our employees often go above and beyond to serve you well. Anyone in particular? _____

8. We sincerely try to resolve all your complaints. _____

9. We make it easy for you to contact us. _____

10. Our employees seem to have a good understanding of all our products and services. _____

11. I would be willing to recommend someone with a need for [your product or service]. _____

In your efforts to gain a profitable stream of referrals, consider reviewing the following three questions discussed in this chapter:

1. Have you taken time to develop relationships?
2. Do people have something unique to talk about?
3. Are you truly referable?

In your answers, you will most likely gain awareness of potential directions you can take for increasing referrals. It's simple, but certainly not easy!

The Employee Connection

The Critical Factor in Creating Clients for Life

I f you asked your staff to work for free, buy their own supplies, or
sell their personal possessions to help you make payroll, they
probably would quickly consider looking for other places to
work. But, this actually—and famously—took place back in 1974,
when a company leader and entrepreneur inspired his employees to
choose to work for free, pay for gas to fuel company trucks with
their personal money, and sell their watches and jewelry to help
the company when all signs were that the business should just fold.
How on Earth could something like this happen, you might
wonder?

Fred Smith is the visionary entrepreneur and founder of Federal
Express who made this a possibility. Smith was often referred to as a
"business evangelist," whose employees would—and *did*—follow
him through thick or thin. He conveyed great power and emotion
to his employees; he gave them a reason to believe, a sense of belonging to something big, and a path to follow. He used his radiant
passion for the business to first create loyal employees, who treated
the company as their own, and then to develop equally loyal

clients, as the passion for overnight delivery spread from one group to the other.

In addition to managing FedEx, Smith is also a co-owner of the Washington Redskins NFL team and owns or co-owns several entertainment companies, including Dream Image Productions and Alcon Films. He was inducted into the Junior Achievement U.S. Business Hall of Fame in 1998 and was presented with the 2008 Kellogg Award for Distinguished Leadership by the Kellogg School of Management. However, none of these accolades, business ventures, or the mark Smith left on the industry of overnight delivery would have come to fruition in the way that it did without the relationship he built with his employees first—one by one. And he didn't establish just *any* relationship; he actually created an environment where they were part of a functional business family where members would do anything for each other.

Building a Client Connection Begins with the Employee Connection

In the 1980s, *Fortune* magazine published a series of articles on America's 10 toughest bosses, all of whom managed in a style that used intimidation and threats. Robert Malott, CEO of the large Chicago manufacturer FMC, declared, "Leadership is demonstrated when the ability to inflict pain is confirmed." While at the time, this statement won Malott quite a few fans, it would likely horrify employees and leadership experts today. CEOs nowadays understand the new dynamics and command power, but exert it through intellect and inspiration.[1]

The Hawthorne Studies on Employee Productivity

The Hawthorne Studies were conducted from 1927 to 1932 at the Western Electric Hawthorne Works in Cicero, Illinois, where Harvard professor Elton Mayo examined productivity and work conditions. Mayo started these experiments by examining the physical and environmental influences of the workplace, and later moved into the psychological aspects. He first set out to study the effect of lighting on productivity by dividing workers into two groups. For the test group, he increased the illumination in their work area. Productivity went up. For the control group, he left the lighting the same, and productivity also went up.

This didn't make sense to Mayo, so he tried another study. He took a group of female employees and gave them regularly scheduled rest times, company paid lunches, and shorter work weeks. Productivity went up. Eighteen months later, all those perks were eliminated, yet productivity *continued* to increase!

After years of running studies relating to employee productivity, four general conclusions were drawn from the Hawthorne studies:

- *The aptitudes of individuals are imperfect predictors of job performance.* Although they give some indication of the physical and mental potential of the individual, the amount produced is strongly influenced by social factors.

- *Informal organization affects productivity. The Hawthorne researchers discovered a group life among the workers.* The studies also showed that the relations that supervisors develop with workers tend to influence the manner in which the workers carry out directives.

- *Work-group norms affect productivity.* The Hawthorne researchers were not the first to recognize that work groups tend to arrive at norms of what is "a fair day's work"; however, they provided the best systematic description and interpretation of this phenomenon.

- *The workplace is a social system.* The Hawthorne researchers came to view the workplace as a social system made up of interdependent parts.

The study found that overall—almost regardless of the experimental manipulation—worker production seemed to *continually improve*. Mayo's experiments showed that an increase in employee efficiency came as the result of the psychological stimulus that being singled out, involved, and made to feel important evoked. Mayo concluded, therefore, that productivity increased every time attention was paid to workers.[2]

What is Different Today?

As it relates to how employees feel and their resulting productivity, nothing has changed from the time of the Hawthorne Studies to today. But in order to motivate, organizations that inspire productivity and retain good employees are looking anew at their staff today. Instead of attempting to fit their workforce into a previously established box, they are creating a new, more open set of workplace rules and conditions. The result is a business structure that takes relationships into account—and that is proving to be a significant win for the employees, the companies, and their customers.

Vineet Nayar is the CEO of HCL Technologies Ltd., a leading global IT services company. HCL has more than 55,000 professionals spread across 20 countries with current annual revenues of $ 2 billion. Vineet's focus has been on creating an organization that is based on an "Employee First, Customer Second" approach and initiative. This results-oriented philosophy takes a contrarian approach to the traditional "customer-first" thinking. Both Harvard Business School and University of Virginia's Darden School of Business have created case studies around the functioning of HCL Technologies.

Vineet insists that creating relationships and connecting is based on the value that others receive. "People are connected because of the value you deliver. Connecting occurs at a 'what are you doing for me' value level." He explains that a connection with customers occurs in the "Value Zone," where people connect with what matters most to them. In order to achieve this, there needs to be a bond between a company and its employees first. "Customers are looking for value not relationships," Vineet says.

"Value *creates* relationships because it is the interface between employee and customer."

HCL's "Employee First, Customer Second" Initiative

To integrate the Employee First initiative, HCL developed four "Employee First, Customer Second" strategic objectives:

1. To provide a unique employee environment.
2. To drive an inverted organizational structure.
3. To create transparency and accountability in the organization.
4. To encourage a value-driven culture.

"From the start, I was clear," Vineet said. "Employee First was not about free lunch, free buses, and subsidies. It was about setting clear priorities, investing in employees' development, and unleashing their potential to produce bottom-line results."

Communication

The HCL Employee First initiative included a vehicle for communication between Vineet and his employees. The objective was to create an environment of trust, transparency, and management accountability through open communication. Employees were encouraged to pose questions (100 per week) to Vineet, which, to this day, he answers and posts for all to view. Vineet commented, "I threw open the door and invited criticism. We were becoming honest, and that was the sign of a healthy company."

"Directions" Meetings

Another Employee First initiative was to launch a series of onsite town hall–type meetings with employees in all of HCL's locations. This gave them an opportunity to voice their opinions, ask questions, and see how they fit into the big picture of the company. As a result, there was an open environment that promoted trust.

Trust Pay

An additional critical change that was made for employees took place when HCL moved from a pay system with performance-based bonuses to what it referred to as "trust pay." This was instituted for 85 percent of employees, most of whom were junior engineers. It did not include senior management and sales. "Trust pay" meant that an employee's entire compensation amount would be fixed, instead of a more typical arrangement of a salary plus bonus based on internal business targets (that, in most companies, are infrequently reached). HCL would, in essence, pay employees in advance for their bonuses and trust that the employee would deliver. It was unheard of in business! But it was intended to reduce transaction volume and increase trust, which it *did*. And perhaps most important, it served to re-energize the company.

The 360° Feedback—For All to See

Then, beginning in 2005, the company announced that all managers would receive 360° feedback for development. In an unprecedented move, Vineet claimed that he would post his 360° feedback on the intranet for all HCL employees to view. Other managers followed suit. This process turned out to be difficult for many managers who were not accustomed to such exposure of information. Vineet said, "When thousands of employees all over the world had the chance to view their top management transparently, I think the message really got across for the first time that we were truly a different company. The transformation process was becoming less dictatorial and more consultative."

Overall, the "Employee First, Customer Second" initiative rejuvenated HCL. The company is gaining market share, and under Vineet's leadership, HCL has grown to 2.5 times its original size over the past three years. Value is now being delivered by committed employees who are interacting and creating powerful relationships with customers.

Command and Control versus Collaboration and Teamwork

Since the 1920s, studies have shown that connections with employees boost productivity. But the playing field has been altered since that time. The principles are the same, but the people have changed. In order to relate to, motivate, and improve productivity, a relationship-oriented management style is emerging.

The "command and control" structure of management does not produce the same results as it once did. The "Y Generation" has a very different set of expectations of management style. Vineet insightfully compared it to the evolution of the family unit. "Today, the family is a collaborative enterprise. Children have a say. That's how the family unit functions now. There is a conversion on core values. Our model in business must be the same or it will not work."

Command and control methods with employees are giving way to more collaborative approaches. Some of the most successful companies in the world are stepping down from formal authority and moving into the encouragement of collaboration, open communication, trust, and interdependencies. Leaders in these companies are building a "leading from behind" perspective.

CEO of Cisco John Chambers discussed in February 2009 the gradual and transforming changes that have been occurring at his company over the past six years. In an interview with Harvard Business School Publishing, Chambers noted that Cisco has moved from a command and control style of management to one of collaboration and teamwork. "We have built our whole structure and evolved our leadership team to do this," Chambers said. "I think the stumbling block we all trip on is that we've been successful with command and control, and therefore, we know how to do it very well. And so my tendency is, when I get in a meeting, to say that it will be collaborative, but within 10 minutes, I know what the answer is, and [I find myself saying], 'Alright, here is where we're going to go.' And you have to let the team get through that and give them the time to come to the right conclusion. And by the way, within a very short time period, they usually make as good or better decisions than I would."

When employees are involved in a spirit of collaboration, their inclusion in processes and decisions brings positive consequences. Individuals naturally crave a level of attention (Hawthorne Studies) and emotional satisfaction (see Chapter 2 on social intelligence), and collaboration gives them that. But it also allows employees to push back and challenge ideas and methods. When all is said and done, the employees are a part of owning decisions and thus are more committed to implementation and success.

A collaborative model of business doesn't simply produce happy and productive employees. It produces satisfied and delighted customers and a sustainable model for business growth.

Two-Way Communication

Communication is in its most effective form when it is going two ways. Employees and managers need ways to exchange ideas and feedback on a regular basis. And, it may no longer be through the "suggestion box" method.

Even in today's high-tech environment, people still seek personal contact. They want to know what the company's future plans are, how they fit in, and understand how things affect them. Many of the award-winning best places to work have leaders who use the managing by walking around (MBWA) principle, believing that potential problems can be quickly solved by talking directly to the individuals involved. It is also a great way to stay in touch with what's really happening in the organization.

Open Lines of Communication

Open communication is a key to creating a sustainable workplace culture, and it is one of the most difficult qualities to master.

According to Winning Workplaces, a not-for-profit group that provides consulting and training for small and midsize organizations, an organization achieves shared trust and the focus on achievement only when communication remains a central tenet of its culture.

American Electric Power (AEP) is one of the largest electric utility providers in the United States, and has taken many steps toward keeping their employees informed and engaged. AEP stays connected with employees through an Intranet site ("AEPNow") that provides tools, information, and resources; a monthly employee newsletter ("Inside AEP") that is mailed home to ensure they communicate with all employees; quarterly employee webcasts scheduled around earnings announcements; and other specialized communications.

In 2007, AEP launched an internal blog that allows employees to sound off on a range of issues important to them. "Open Mike" is another employee forum that meets privately and regularly with the CEO. Participation in Open Mike rotates to allow for broader participation; 25 employees are part of this program each year.

In the Hawthorne Studies conducted 80 years ago, Elton Mayo concluded that productivity increased every time he paid attention to workers. Today, if the same study was done, it would perhaps be found that human nature hasn't changed all that much.

CHAPTER 12

I Don't Have Time to Connect!

Finding the Time to Connect with an Already Busy Schedule

Time is a fixed income and, as with any income, the real problem facing most of us is how to live successfully within our daily allotment.

—Margaret B. Johnstone

Where have you heard this before? "My schedule is already filled to overflowing. How in the world am I supposed to find time to make connections, to build relationships?"

How often have you said it yourself? "I don't have time!" We're living in the Age of Technology, but it seems that all the tools at our disposal—which were supposed to help us make better use of our time—have only caused us to become increasingly busier.

We're living in what might be more accurately called The Age of Overload. Trying to find the time to do all the things that clamor for our attention is one of the burning issues of the day. Do an online search of the word "time," and you'll get nearly six *billion* results! Narrow your search to "time management," and you've cut that number to a little more than 200 million. Narrow it still further by putting quotation marks around those two words ("time management") and you're down to a mere 15 million or so.

Included in these results are tips, tools, tests, and tricks; plans, proverbs, and principles; secrets, solutions, strategies, systems, studies, and skills. There are time management seminars and workshops, counseling and coaching services, speeches to listen to and videos to watch. There's literally something for everyone: time management for kids, teenagers, and college students; for women and families; for teachers, pastors, businesspeople, and the chronically disorganized. And—just in case you've simply been too busy to find time to overthrow the government—there's at least one web site that offers time management advice for anarchists!

So, with all these tools and all this advice at our disposal, how come we keep running out of time? Perhaps we can find one answer in the writings of the late Peter F. Drucker, who was often called "the father of modern management" and who devoted a significant amount of his teaching and writing to the importance of this topic.

"Time," Drucker wrote, "is always in short supply. There is no substitute for time. Everything requires time. It is the only truly universal condition. All work takes place in, and uses up time. Yet most people take for granted this unique, irreplaceable and necessary resource."

Drucker's assertion has only become more valid as time has passed. There are various ways that we take time for granted. We may succumb to what's been called "the tyranny of the urgent," wherein we allow relatively unimportant interruptions—emails, phone calls, unannounced visits—to use some of our allotment of time. In the words of contemporary American author and newspaper columnist Antoinette Bosco, "Time isn't a commodity, something you pass around like cake. Time is the substance of life. When anyone asks you to give your time, they're really asking for a chunk of your life."

Something else that keeps many of us from making the best use of our time is the "P" word—procrastination. Famed English author Charles Dickens called it "the thief of time," and the late American author and humorist Don Marquis described it as "the art of keeping up with yesterday." Miguel de Cervantes, the sixteenth century Spanish novelist, poet, and author of the acclaimed *Don Quixote*, sounded this warning about procrastination: "By the streets of by and by, one arrives at the house of never."

A third and perhaps the most significant factor that keeps us from making the best use of our time is a lack of organization—a failure to plan or to establish priorities. The Roman poet known as Ovid once noted that "Time flies." And, in the 2,000 or so years since then, millions of people have made that same lament. But now motivational speaker Michael Altshuler has given it a new twist: "The bad news is that time flies. The good news is that you're the pilot."

The following stories demonstrate how you, as the pilot, can take the controls of your ship of time, guiding it to the most productive and profitable destinations.

Simple but Sound Advice

Unless public relations is your specialty, the name Ivy Ledbetter Lee probably won't mean anything. Born in Georgia in 1877, he later graduated from Princeton University and began working as a newspaper reporter. In 1904, Lee and a partner launched a practice in the brand new field of public relations. In fact, Lee is considered by many as the father of modern public relations.

His clients included some of the best-known business titans of the day—John D. Rockefeller, Jr. and Charles M. Schwab, for example. In 1903, after serving as president of Carnegie Steel

Company and then U.S. Steel Corporation, Schwab took the reins at Bethlehem Steel Corporation, the nation's then-second largest steel producer. On one occasion, Schwab spoke to Lee, who was serving as a PR consultant to the company, about how his managers might make more effective use of their time.

Almost immediately, Lee scribbled out a simple plan, suggested that Schwab put it into practice for a time, and then pay him for whatever the steel executive thought the advice was worth. The plan proved to be so effective that Schwab sent Lee a check in the amount of $25,000, the equivalent of perhaps a quarter of a million dollars today.

What sort of a plan was worth that much money? It consisted of four simple steps:

1. Make a list of the most important things you have to do tomorrow.
2. Arrange them in the order of their importance (prioritize them).
3. The next day work on the most important task until it's completed.
4. Tackle the other tasks in priority order.

More than a century later, this still remains sound advice for effectively managing one's time.

"All We Have"

Randy Pausch, PhD, a computer science professor at Pittsburgh's Carnegie Mellon University, believed passionately in the importance of managing one's time. "Time management makes you figure out what's important and what's not," he said. "Time is all we have. You may find one day that you have less than you think."

That "one day" in Pausch's life came on August 15, 2007, when he was told by his doctors that his pancreatic cancer, first discovered a year earlier, had reached the point where he had only three to six months to live. In fact, he lived for nearly another year, finally succumbing to his disease on July 25, 2008. He was 47 years old, and he left behind his wife, Jai, and three small children, ages 2, 3, and 6.

Asked during those final months if his view about time had changed, Pausch said the only difference was that "everything now is more so." He was more determined than ever to make every minute count and to leave his wife and children with lasting memories. For example, there were romantic getaways with Jai and family trips to Disneyland.

In September 2007, Pausch took part in a Carnegie Mellon lecture series in which faculty members had been asked to deliver hypothetical "last lectures," except that, in his case, there was nothing hypothetical about it. Titled "Really Achieving Your Childhood Dreams," his lecture, which he said was aimed primarily at his children, swept the world and has been downloaded from the Internet several million times.

Newspapers all across the country picked up the story; Pausch appeared on "Oprah" and other TV shows. In November 2007, the University of Virginia, where Pausch had taught for a decade before moving to Carnegie Mellon, asked him to come and deliver an updated version of a message he had delivered there in 1998. The subject, of course, was time management.

In it he shared his concepts and practices for using time most effectively. They included many of the tried and true principles of time management: planning and goal setting; establishing priorities; maintaining to-do lists; doing the "ugliest" things first; handling every piece of paper and every email just once; and learning to say "No." He recommended keeping phone calls short by making them near the end of the workday or just before lunchtime. "You may think you're important," he said, "but you're not as important as lunch."

Throughout his message, which was accompanied by a slide presentation, Pausch's sense of humor was continually on display. For instance, when speaking about the importance of delegation as a time saver, and insisting that it's never too soon to begin the practice, he showed a slide of two nearly identical photos of himself holding his infant daughter on his lap. The only difference was, in one photo, Pausch is holding the bottle; in the other, the baby is holding it herself.

Just as with his "last lecture," Randy Pausch's lecture on time management has been seen and heard countless times; both of these and other Pausch messages remain available online at www.randy pausch.com.

Big Rocks First

In his book about time management, *First Things First*, best-selling author Stephen R. Covey relates a story told by one of his associates about a seminar in which the presenter conducted an experiment that powerfully illustrated the principles espoused by Ivy Lee, Randy Pausch, and others.

Setting a large Mason jar on the table in front of him, he proceeded to place in it fist-sized rocks until the jar could hold no more. When he asked his audience if the jar was full, they all replied, "Yes."

He then produced a bag of gravel and poured as much of it as he could into the jar. When he again asked if the jar was full, the answer this time was "Probably not."

He next poured as much sand into the jar as it would hold, and repeated his question. The audience response was a resounding "No."

The final step was to add water until the jar was truly full. Then he asked the group to explain the point of the illustration. One person's quick response was that you can always figure out how to squeeze more things into your life.

"No," the speaker replied, "that's not the point. What this illustration teaches us is if you don't put the big rocks in first, you'll never be able to get them in at all."

What are the big rocks—the priorities—in your life, personally and professionally? That's a good question to ask yourself about everything that demands a portion of your time. If becoming a connector and building relationships is important to you, you'd be wise to put that big rock into your jar of time before it gets filled with the little things. Guard against those pebbles of interruption, those grains of unimportant time-wasting tasks, the procrastination that fills your jar of time to overflowing.

Finally, heed this advice and this warning sounded by English author and poet John Dryden some four centuries ago: "Time is the most valuable coin in your life. You and you alone will determine how that coin will be spent. Be careful that you don't let other people spend it for you."

Resource

For more information on strategies for managing your time in order to achieve your priorities and find time for connections, please see Chapter 20, "Coaching Your Way through to Better Relationships: A Self-Coaching Exercise for Improving Business Relationships."

13

Find a Mentor

The Influence that Leads, Motivates and Holds You Accountable

You need mentors in your life to take you to the places you want to go!!! Why do you need mentors? Well, it's simple. Mentors cause you to change, or stretch yourself to new limits not known before. They also give you a larger vision for your life than you can see for yourself.

—Tom Pace

In practice, the mentoring process has been around for hundreds of years. In fact, the word "mentor" is derived from ancient Greek mythology. According to legend, when Odysseus went off to war he gave a man named Mentor the responsibility of looking after his young son. The word has since come to mean one who functions as a counselor, advisor, or guide to another.

The mentor-mentee relationship is typically one of an older to younger person, or a more experienced person to a less experienced one. It's often been expressed in the vernacular as "taking someone under your wing."

While the custom of mentoring isn't new, it's evolved into a formal business practice in recent years. Recognizing their value as a training tool and for enhancing relationships, more and more large corporations have adopted mentoring programs that engage new employees as soon as they're hired. In fact, according to a January 29, 2009, article in *The Wall Street Journal*, some 70 percent of Fortune 500 companies now provide mentoring programs. As an example, the article cites International Business Machines (IBM), where "every employee is assigned a 'connection coach' before their first day; after they join, workers are assigned a formal mentor."

In its simplest form, mentoring is the process of people helping people. It is a relationship where one person assists in the personal and professional development of another. When asked, most notably successful businesspeople will tell you that at one time, they had or still have a mentor. It is a real key to the successful growth of a businessperson. This mentor-mentee connection is also valuable because it teaches the mentee the basics of a strong relationship: giving and getting.

So, Do You Have a Mentor?

Below is a worksheet that has been helpful to those interested in starting a mentor-mentee relationship.

Downloadable Form 13.1: Choosing a Mentor

1. What characteristics am I looking for in a mentor?

    _____

    _____

    _____

    _____

    _____

    _____

2. What do I want to accomplish with my mentor relationship?

_____

_____

_____

_____

_____

_____

3. What skills do I need to improve?

_____

_____

_____

_____

_____

4. Who are potential mentors for me?

_____

_____

_____

_____

_____

You can also access a free download of this worksheet, "Choosing a Mentor" at www.redzonemarketing.com/TheConnectors. Enter keycode "CONNECT" to download it for free!

The Mentee: What to Expect

An April 15, 2002, article on the IBM web site entitled "Mentor capital: Growing a company's most precious resource" describes the many benefits of a corporate mentoring program. In it, author and Director of Professional Services Sidney E. Fuchs offers sound advice for those seeking to be mentored. "Not everyone," he writes, "is a prime candidate for *being* mentored. When you link up with a coach, you must be willing to open yourself to constructive feedback, face reality, and attack the hard stuff. On the plus side, this can lead to achieving your goals and making remarkable improvements."

Having been in a similar role himself earlier in his career, Fuchs speaks from experience. He points out that for the relationship to be successful, the mentee must be willing to be open, to tackle the most difficult issues first, and to be prepared to accept what can be painful criticism at times. "After that," he writes, "the rest is much easier. Opening up and letting someone you trust dig, pry, and inject a dose of reality into your world is very liberating. If they're doing it for the right reasons, it can make a critical difference in your career."

A Mentoring Event

Many organizations and events have moved beyond just networking to create and facilitate the mentor-mentee relationship. CEO Space, Inc. (www.ibiglobal.com), cofounded by BJ Dohrmann, hosts five annual CEO retreat weeks and has an online community for CEOs.

BJ's father, Alan G. Dohrmann, coached and trained some of the most revered businesspeople from the 1940s through the 1970s. The younger Dohrmann grew up amongst successful businesspeople and learned from them and his father on how to successfully network and connect with people of power.

CEO Space acts much like a unique trade show for CEO-to-CEO cross mentorship. The goal of each retreat week is to lower the cost and time to complete near-term planning objectives. CEO Space retreat weeks employ a unique "CEO pacing" such that every 90 minutes leaders at the top move into generous break periods to manage email, phone, and related responsibilities. CEOs receive a current download of classic MBA skill refresher training.

The Xerox Approach

In 1984, Xerox Corporation launched a program called The Women's Alliance (TWA) with the mission of serving as "a catalyst to advance the personal and professional development of women at

Xerox, enabling each of us to attain our goals." More recently, TWA incorporated a mentoring program as an additional means of aiding in both the personal and professional growth of its members. The TWA web site (www.thewomensalliance.net) describes the mentoring program as "facilitated by a web-based tool where mentees enter in the preference for areas of expertise and receive a list of potential mentors. The mentee then establishes and maintains a relationship with the mentor of choice."

The web-based tool also includes profiles of available mentors and the answers to key questions for mentees on topics such as dealing with finding the right mentor, how often to meet, expectations for both mentee and mentor, when and how to end a mentorship, plus which areas to discuss and which to consider avoiding.

A TWA brochure about the program cites a report from *Business Finance Magazine* (2000) that revealed the following:

- 71 percent of Fortune 500 and private companies use mentoring.
- 34 percent of women executives and 24 percent of CEOs pointed to a lack of mentoring as one of the most significant obstacles for women.
- Employees who have mentors earn between $5,610–$22,450 (U.S.) more a year than employees who do not have mentors.
- 77 percent of U.S. companies surveyed said that mentoring improved both retention and performance of employees.

The same TWA brochure defines superior mentoring relationships as "partnerships with both mentor and mentee learning, developing, and deriving satisfaction from working together. Mentees must be proactive in the mentoring process, setting goals and asking questions."

Approaching Potential Mentors

It can be a nerve-wracking thing to approach a potential mentor. What if they say no? What if I make them feel uncomfortable? What if I feel uncomfortable?

Here are some examples of how others have initiated conversations with potential mentors:

1. *Referral.* Ask someone to introduce you to a person with whom you'd like to begin a mentor-mentee relationship. Give them all the reasons why you are seeking this particular person out.

2. *Email/Phone/Face-to-Face.* Try approaching them via one of these means in the following way: "I have admired your career and know that you are someone who has a lot of experience in _____. I was wondering if you would be willing to give me some advice?"

An Unlikely Mentoring Champion

I began this chapter with a quote by a man named Tom Pace about the importance of mentoring relationships. My guess is that you've never heard of him; until recently, I hadn't either. Then I had an opportunity to read his story, and it's truly an amazing one.

Born in 1957, Pace showed little—if any—promise of making anything productive out of his life. In high school, for example, his grades earned him mostly Cs, Ds, and Fs. By the time he graduated, he was—by his own admission—a functional illiterate, reading at about the fourth-grade level.

Pace then made what can best be described as a half-hearted attempt at continuing his "education," first at the University of Oklahoma, then on to Oklahoma State University and finally to the University of Central Oklahoma, where he barely got by, skipped classes altogether, and then finally dropped out.

His work record was no better; he estimates that by the time he was in his mid-twenties, he'd held, and lost, close to 30 jobs. "In 1983," he said, "I had hit rock bottom"; he even contemplated suicide.

But instead, Pace did something that seems out of character for a man who could barely read. Someone told him about a book titled *The Greatest Miracle in the World*, by Og Mandino, and he read it. Mandino, it turned out, was a kindred spirit who had also made a mess of his early life. "I was a drunk," he says, "a 35-year-old bum, ready to end it all. I had thirty dollars in my pocket, and when I saw a gun in a pawnshop for twenty-nine dollars, I almost bought it."

Mandino, of course, went on to become one of the most widely read inspirational authors in the world. By the time of his death in 1996, his 14 books had sold more than 50 million copies in 25 languages. What had changed his life? It was a motivational book he had chanced to read, just as Tom Pace would.

Mandino's words in *The Greatest Miracle in the World* would have a tremendous impact on Pace: "You are capable of great wonders. Your potential is unlimited . . . Never demean yourself again! Never settle for the crumbs of life! Never hide your talents, from this day hence!"

Reading soon became Tom Pace's passion; it awakened in him long-suppressed dreams of what his future would hold. In 1987, at age 30, after his string of job failures and with a grand total of $62.53 to his name, he decided to start his own business. And so Pace/Butler Corporation was born. At first, it specialized in buying and reselling used computer equipment and later used cell phones. Over the years, Tom has grown the company into a profitable multi-milliondollar business employing more than 100 workers.

Today, everything Tom Pace does is based on his commitment to make the world a better place. At the heart of it is his passion for mentoring, which led him to launch a nonprofit organization named MentorHope, LLC (www.mentorhope.com). And, in 2007, with co-author Walter Jenkins, he wrote MENTOR: *The Kid & The CEO, A Simple Story of Overcoming Challenges and Achieving Significance.* Published by Mentor Hope Publishing, the book tells the story of a young man named Tony who, while still in his teens, had several run-ins with the law and whose life was going nowhere. Then he met a successful businessman who mentored him and changed his life. Pace dedicated the book "to all those who cared enough to mentor me."

Pace conveys a lot of important information about mentoring. First, he points out that there are two types of mentors: direct and indirect. The latter category includes people with whom we have no direct contact, but whose wisdom and guidance are available to everyone through books, tapes, seminars, and other resources. In fact, Pace considers habits like reading to be such an important part of the mentoring process that, years ago, he launched a program designed to encourage his Pace/Butler employees to become readers. For every non-fiction book of 100 pages or more that an employee reads, he or she receives $10. Since the program began employees have read thousands of books on a wide range of topics, including self-improvement, child-rearing, finances, and spiritual matters. Because of one particular employee's suggestion, a list of all books read is posted and, during weekly staff meetings, employees have become comfortable sharing some of the positive influences their reading has had on them.

As successful as that program has been, Pace is quick to point out that direct mentoring is the more effective approach. "Direct mentors," he writes, "are people with whom you can actually sit down and schedule a time to meet. This is the most effective method of mentoring, because [it allows you] to see the mentor in action. You should take advantage of both methods, with your main focus on direct mentoring."

I began this chapter with Tom Pace's explanation of *why* having a mentor is important. Let me conclude with his words of wisdom on *how* to begin developing that relationship:

"Choose the strengths of different people to build the qualities in your life you want to enhance. Find individuals who have already accomplished your purpose. Make sure they are available and accessible.

"Now, here is the most important part of being mentored that a lot of people miss. You have to know how to find help from your mentor. If you are not prepared for your time with your mentor, you are wasting your time. If you don't know what you want from your mentor, you will never know if you are progressing or not . . .

"Remember, a mentor is the most important ingredient for success that you can have in your life. Work hard, stay focused, get mentored and have fun!!!"

Downloadable Form 13.2: Mentor Meeting Checklist

1. What do I want to accomplish?

_____

_____

_____

_____

2. What are the skills, in priority, that I need to learn?

_____

_____

_____

_____

3. What specific questions will I ask?

_____

_____

_____

_____

4. How will I take action after the mentor-mentee meeting? When?

_____

_____

_____

_____

5. How will I follow up with the mentor on actions? How often?

_____

_____

_____

_____

6. When would I like to meet again?

_____

_____

_____

_____

For more information about the advantages of mentoring, including a helpful tool for use in finding a mentor and meeting with your mentor ("The Mentor Meeting Checklist"), go to www .redzonemarkting.com/theconnectors. Enter keycode "CONNECT" to download it for free!

CHAPTER 14

Women's Organizations

Fulfilling a Unique Need for Women to Connect

Continue developing and expanding your network . . . I firmly believe that behind every successful woman is a huge network, one she has built by meeting new people.

—Sandra Yancey

T
he seeds of what would become the first organization in the United States to champion the needs and goals of women in business and the professions were planted in time of war. Beginning in 1914, what was then called The Great War had been raging across Europe. By 1917, it had escalated to the point where U.S. involvement became unavoidable, and on April 6 of that same year, the U.S. Congress formally declared war on Germany. Four million young American men were quickly drafted and, by the following summer, were being sent overseas at the rate of 10,000 per day.

As the mobilization of increasing numbers of men thinned the ranks of America's workforce, U.S. War Department officials saw the need to identify and coordinate the resources of professional and business women. A Women's War Council was established, which led to the founding of The National Federation of Business and Professional Women's Club on July 15, 1919. The name was later changed to Business and Professional Women/USA—often called simply BPW/USA—and its stated mission is to "achieve equity for all women in the workplace through advocacy, education, and information."

As described on its web site (www.bpwusa.org), BPW/USA is "a national grassroots organization, [with] 20,000 members, 1,300 local organizations in 54 states and U.S. territories . . . BPW members are working women seeking to advance their career goals, earn higher salaries, build stronger business, achieve pay equity and equal opportunities, and establish rewarding careers."

During the past 90 years, much of the organization's focus has been on legislative issues affecting women, and its dedicated efforts have resulted in significant success. At the same time, it has never lost sight of the need to build relationships and make important connections. Quoting again from the organization's web site: "BPW/USA's commitment to America's working women is reflected in our signature conferences, events and programming. These important tools communicate the core values of BPW and provide connections nationally as women learn from one another, support each other, lobby and create lifelong networks."

Each year, for example, BPW/USA hosts its national conference, where hundreds of women from all across America gather to attend professional development workshops and take advantage of career coaching opportunities, while they network and develop important connections. In 1956, the organization formed the Business and Professional Women's Foundation, with the mission to "empower working women to achieve their full potential and to partner with employers to build successful workplaces."

Not long ago, BPW/USA reached out to the rapidly growing number of America's women veterans by launching "Women Joining Forces: Closing Ranks, Opening Doors." Its purpose is to help ease women's transition from military to civilian life through a variety of programs and services, including job and scholarship opportunities and other resources specifically for women veterans. A key component of this program involves connections—providing these veterans with access to the kinds of relationships that will help ease the transition from their military careers to civilian employment and success.

NAWBO

While BPW/USA is the nation's oldest women's business organization, it is by no means the only one dedicated to helping business and professional women build strategic connections and key relationships. Another such organization is the National Association of Women Business Owners, better known simply as NAWBO.

Founded in 1975 in Washington, D.C. by a dozen businesswomen, NAWBO now has chapters in nearly every major metropolitan area, and represents more than 10 million women-owned businesses. Its four-pronged mission includes strengthening the wealth-creating capacity of its members and promoting economic development; creating innovative and effective change in the business culture; transforming public policy and influencing opinion makers; and building strategic alliances, coalitions, and affiliations.

NAWBO's efforts to help its members make valuable connections and develop key relationships to foster the growth of their individual enterprises includes its affiliation with several other organizations with similar goals. For example, through its affiliation with Les Femmes Chef d'Enterprises Mondiales (translation: World Association of Women Entrepreneurs), its global reach now extends to 60 countries on five continents. Simply stated, FCEM's mission is "linking women business owners the world over."

In 2004, NAWBO formed an alliance with Count Me In for Women's Economic Independence. The mission of this not-for-profit organization is "to promote economic independence and the growth of women owned businesses." Since its founding in 1999, Count Me In has made hundreds of loans to women-owned ventures in all 50 states.

With the assistance of NAWBO, a new organization—the Network of Entrepreneurial Women Worldwide (NEWWW)—was launched in 2006. According to World President Christine Chauvet, "In a global and permanently mutating economical context, it is important to strengthen exchanges and partnerships. Already represented among the five continents, NEWWW gathers associations of women entrepreneurs, dynamic in their own countries."

Within its own ranks, NAWBO has also been busy expanding its role on behalf of business and professional women. In 2003, it formed the NAWBO Institute for Entrepreneurial Development, a not-for-profit educational foundation "that seeks to provide opportunities for capacity building and organizational development for emerging and established women entrepreneurs."

Women's Leadership Exchange® (WLE)

The WLE mission is to provide the knowledge, tools, and connections women need to be successful in their own businesses, the corporate world, and the not-for-profit environment. A progressive organization formed in 2001, WLE is a social entrepreneurship organization founded by and for businesswomen. WLE acknowledges the unique challenges facing women in business, whether they are leading their own companies or are leaders in the corporate, government, or not-for-profit sectors. To meet these challenges, they offer programs that help women fill the information gap and provide a venue for building connections to facilitate their success in business and in life.

WLE hosts a plethora of conferences across the United States that feature leading experts, accredited executive coaches, and interactive programming. WLE also offers many resources for businesswomen on their web site, through teleconferences, an e-newsletter, local presentations, and a facilitated connection program that enables women to lend support to each other locally and nationally. The group was founded by entrepreneurs Leslie Grossman and Andrea March. As owner of a leading NYC marketing/PR firm in the 1990s,

Leslie Grossman was responsible for the eight-year campaign that brought platinum jewelry back from the dead to become the preferred metal for brides all over the United States. Her marketing-to-women strategy evolved into a focus on businesswomen as a result of her experience as a leader of many women's business associations, including serving as president of NAWBO, NYC and NY Chair of the Women's Leadership Forum (a division of the DNC). Grossman has been active for many years in the small business and women's business communities.

Andrea March reinvented herself several times as a woman business owner and leader. After selling real estate for some years, she and her husband launched a jewelry import and distribution company, Andrea March Accessories. March, who had always had a passion for jewelry, was the salesperson as well as the designer for this affordable line of costume jewelry. The couple ran their multi-million dollar business together for 20 years. Then, while watching a program on CNBC, March realized that she had no idea what topic the show was covering and wanted to do something about it. Like many others, Andrea says, "I did not understand investing, and was probably not the exception; there were undoubtedly millions of people like me, with money to invest and no understanding of how to make smart decisions."

Thus was born Investment Expo, the largest financial strategies trade show/seminar program in the Northeast attracting up to 14,000 attendees annually. Four years later, in 2001, Andrea met Leslie Grossman, who had attended one of her two-day events. The two experienced women business owners shared a powerful commitment to women entrepreneurs like themselves. That commitment became Women's Leadership Exchange®.

eWomenNetwork

I opened this chapter with a quotation from Sandra Yancey—a truly remarkable woman. Within the last decade, Yancey has built an organization that is playing a significant and rapidly expanding role in helping business and professional women develop strategic relationships. As a first-generation Mexican American, Sandra credits her mother for instilling in her both the traditions of her Hispanic heritage and the courage to follow her dream. Among the childhood lessons she learned from her mother that has stayed with her and helped shape the philosophy that has served her so well is "Give without remembering, and take without forgetting."

A wife and mother herself, Sandra was sitting alone in her office at home in July 1999 when she conceived the idea for what would become eWomenNetwork. She decided to begin by seeking input through a combination of focus groups and research studies. The process took a little more than a year and, as a result, eWomen Network.com, which was comprised of her personal database of 20 women, made its live debut on the Internet on September 18, 2000. Its core philosophy is "It takes teamwork to make a dream work." According to the feedback Yancey had received from women in those focus groups, they didn't have time to attend meetings; so her original plan was to develop just an online networking organization.

However, it wasn't long before the concept of building just an online network changed. In her article "Let's Talk Business, Woman-to-Woman," featured in *Chicken Soup for the Entrepreneur's Soul* (Health Communications, Inc., 2006), she explained what happened: "I discovered that some of our members wanted to meet in person. It was then I realized I had asked the wrong questions to the focus groups; my original question was 'Would you attend another meeting?'"

Yancey quickly expanded her operation by adding what she called "events" (rather than "meetings") while retaining the online networking concept; it gives her members the best of both worlds and allows them to connect in the ways that *they* preferred most. "That shift to incorporate both online and personal networking opportunities for our members," she reported, "created success I could never have anticipated. I definitely learned from my mistake."

And she learned well. Less than a decade later, the Dallas-based eWomenNetwork has become the fastest growing professional women's networking organization in North America. It numbers more than 100 chapters across the United States and Canada, has in excess of 600,000 members, conducts approximately 2,000 networking events for its members annually, and records 200,000 visits to its web site—every day! It ranks as the most visited business women's web site in both the United States and Canada.

"You can have it all, but not without access," says Yancey, who holds a master's degree in organizational development from American University, in Washington, D.C. As a result of her success, she has been profiled in various newspapers and magazines in the United States and Canada, and was named by *Women's Enterprise Magazine* as among the nation's top-five change agents for women and business.

In 2001, Yancey founded the eWomenNetwork Foundation, a not-for-profit affiliate that provides numerous ways for network members to reach out in support of members who are less fortunate than they. Each year, the group presents its International Conference & Business Expo, which highlights the work of the foundation and includes the presentation of its International Femtor Awards. Since its inception, the eWomenNetwork Foundation has presented hundreds of thousands of dollars in cash grants, in-kind donations and support to other women's nonprofit organizations, as well as scholarships for emerging female leaders of tomorrow.

In addition to the challenges and responsibilities of leading the fast-growing organization she founded, Yancey also finds time to host the weekly eWomenNetwork radio show, which originates from the Dallas studios of WBAP News/Talk 820, a major ABC affiliate which has the largest listening audience in Texas. She's also the author of the best-selling *Relationship Networking: The Art of Turning Contacts into Connections*. Its main message is "Behind every successful woman is a network."

When asked how one develops an effective network, Yancey replied, "To establish a growing and evolving relationship with your core constituents, you must first recognize, believe, and behave according to the philosophy of 'It takes teamwork to make the dream work.' It's through the spirit of abundance that you first demonstrate your own character and integrity by helping others wherever you can. After all, how can you expect others to do for you what you are not willing to do for them?"

Based on her experience Yancey is convinced that those who succeed as connectors believe in giving first. "They constantly and consistently look for ways to share contacts, resources, information, and leads, without the expectation of anything in return. They understand the law of the universe; that is, you must give in order to receive. And, you inherently know that when you give freely and without exceptions, you will be rewarded ten-fold."

In my view, that's another way of expressing that long-ago lesson Sandra Yancey learned at her mother's knee: "Give without remembering and take without forgetting."

The Common Theme

While each of these organizations we've described has its own distinct role to play on behalf of its constituents, there is one theme common to all of them. The words may be different—alliances, coalitions, affiliations, links, growth, partnerships, associations—but all add up to a single goal: making connections and developing relationships.

As a female and active member of my community, I have been involved with several women's organizations myself. I have spoken on business and marketing strategies at conferences for WLE, NAWBO, and eWomenNetwork. However, prior to participating in these organizations, most of my experiences in business have been working in fields that are dominated by men. And, I have to admit, I was initially surprised by the sharing and offers of assistance that women in these organizations give to each other. These women's organizations are *truly* purposed for helping women connect better in business.

Perhaps the best statement summarizing the driving force behind these organizations is found on the NAWBO's web site: "We know that no one succeeds alone . . . and NAWBO offers the means for women business owners to contribute to the success of others."

Power Tools for Relationship Building

CHAPTER 15

How to Get the Most from Outlook, ACT, and Other CRM Software

Strategies for Organizing and Tracking Relationships

Please note that this chapter does not include a remedial review of how to use these CRM programs. We are focused on some simple and perhaps unique strategies for doing what we all do everyday— work within these programs and attempt to manage our business relationships.

The key to using any software program is to remember that it is *only a tool*. In order to effectively use any of these CRM (Customer Relationship Management) programs, you must first have an organized strategy. These programs will help, but they will not do the work for you. However, the good news is that, with a little preparation, almost any good CRM program can make managing and staying in touch with your best contacts much easier.

"I have found that organizing my work through CRM technology has given me significant increases in productivity," said Eric M.A. Cima, CFS, and vice president of operations at The Tranel Financial Group in Libertyville, Ill. "But more importantly, it has helped our team become more productive. Our whole business is about communicating with and servicing clients. We depend on the referrals we receive from our delighted clients. We must have the tools in place to do this and manage our client relationships effectively."

Strategies for Organizing Emails

Red Zone Marketing receives so many emails that it is often hard to organize and answer them based on priority, quickly access information about the sender, and simply keep track of all of them. We've found that one of the best ways is to address the emails when you get them by categorizing them for the appropriate action.

Some common folders to create are "Respond later," "Read later," "Subject Category (i.e., Marketing)," and so on. Then you can file emails in the folders you have made. One great time saver is to create a folder called "FYI," for all of the emails on which you've been CC'ed, but upon which you do not need to take action—even though somebody thought you should at least be aware of the subject matter. The only emails that are in your immediate inbox are the ones to which you need to respond right away or the ones you have yet to categorize. You can then schedule 15-minute blocks of time in your day to respond to emails. This process requires self-discipline, but if you don't establish some sort of plan, it is possible to spend almost all of your time responding to the last-in, low-priority emails.

For those of you who have a difficult time with self-discipline but know in your heart what you *should* do, simply delegate this task to your computer. Microsoft Outlook, for example, has great tools like "filter" and "rules" that can automatically perform these functions for you, so that you don't have to think about certain actions once you've established the rules. For example, you can have any email from a certain person and/or a certain subject automatically placed into one of the folders we just mentioned (including the delete folder). You can keep them in your main inbox, but have them appear as a certain color, so that you know which ones are related, and so that you can focus on one topic at a time.

The software that exists today is powerful, and most of us probably only tap into about 20 percent to 30 percent of what it is capable of. Imagine if we learned how to get more out of it, and used 80 percent to 90 percent of what these programs can offer. Learn from those around you, or take some time to attend a class—either online, in a classroom, or through a CD that you purchase. It can take less than an hour to find out about some great tools that will literally save you *hundreds* of hours in the future.

Email Inbox Backwards

Many professionals use Microsoft Outlook to send and receive emails. We have recently heard praises from some connectors about a (free!) application called Xobni that allows you to quickly track relationship information. The San Francisco-based startup's name is the word "inbox" spelled backwards, which serves as an affirmation by the company to "take back" the email inbox for their users. Xobni is an advanced tool that searches for email conversations, attachments, and other important information. I've personally been using it and find it to be a very valuable tool for keeping track of not just emails or contacts, but relationships as well.

One of Xobni's interesting features is that the program creates an individual profile for each person who emails you. These profiles contain relationship statistics, contact information, social media connections, threaded conversations, and shared attachments. Their users tell them that Xobni makes an inbox work the way their mind works. For instance, this application lets me know how quickly I respond to my emails. Denise Peterson who works at Red

Zone Marketing must really be something (she is!) because, on average, I send a response to her emails in *four minutes*. But the most fascinating relationship tool it provides—beyond all of the remarkable analytics—is its ability to conduct a search and provide contact information, access LinkedIn and Facebook profiles, and even photos of the person whose email you're reading. Xobni displays extremely helpful material and other company information on the right side of the computer screen. I love it!

OneNote—Master Organizer

This is a powerful piece of software that helps organize information from many sources and keeps it at your fingertips for exactly when it's needed. OneNote is set up as a digital spiral notebook—a really big one, because you can have as many pages, tabs, and sections as you want. You can actually flip/fan through the pages just like you would a real notebook (yes, just like putting your thumb at the edge of the page and flipping through a book). You can type notes into OneNote, and if you have a tablet-type laptop, you can even hand write on the pages. And the great thing about this tool versus a real notebook is that if you are taking notes and need to go back and add info in the middle of a page or paragraph, you can easily add space to do so. It flows seamlessly in your own handwriting instead of having long lines with arrows at the end pointing to where a note really should be.

In addition to text, you can capture pictures in OneNote (photographs or your own drawings). You can audio and video record onto your notes pages. The latest version even allows you to search the audio for key words. You can create links to pages with any of your notebooks; so you only have to write something once in order to reference that information from multiple places.

OneNote syncs well with Outlook, so you can easily send your emails to a note pages in order to reference them during a meeting. You can set tags to let you know to whom you should delegate work, or to remind you to view a handout or get a book related to your note. You can sort and reference the tags easily, and have them remind you to check the status of work you've already assigned. You can also create tasks for yourself or assign them to someone else from OneNote thru Outlook so that you are able to utilize automatic tracking.

Strategies for Organizing Connections/Contacts

Vice President of Marketing and Business Development at Accu-Quote, a term life insurance quoting firm, Sean Cheyney has developed some simple but effective strategies for organizing the contacts he receives. Cheyney is responsible for spearheading the overall growth and direction of the company's marketing initiatives, strategic partnerships, and customer acquisition. He is also directly responsible for initiating and maintaining all advertising and partnership relationships to help benefit and promote the company's image and business model. So it doesn't come as a surprise that Cheyney has more than his share of contacts to classify.

"When I attend an event, I try to organize a list in advance of those people that will be attending," Cheyney explains. "I color code the list with one color for those people I already know, and another color for people I want to meet. Right after the event, I make notes on my list. Then, that night, I go to LinkedIn and send a personal note and invite the people I met to connect." Indeed, a very simple and effective strategy. Cheyney's relationships will then move forward, based on the responses that are received, the other person's willingness to connect, and the opportunity to meet again. Cheyney says, "I also look for opportunities to help the other person by connecting them to people I know."

And, to take it to the next level of organization, the contact information is entered into the CRM database program.

Four Tips for Organizing Connections

1. **Entering basic information into the database**
   - Enter name, address, phone, cell, email, social media links, and web site.

2. Entering notes and key personal information
   - Do this while the information is still fresh in your mind. Otherwise, the info you put in could be incorrect, and garbage in means garbage out (GIGO) for the accountants reading this book
   - Record the important and remarkable facts
   - Capture the spirit of the meeting/call

3. Scheduling activities
   - Schedule a follow-up after every contact you have with someone
   - Drag an email right to your tasks so you don't have to write the information again or copy and paste

4. Weekly lists to run
   - List of phone calls from previous week
   - List of scheduled activities for the current week
   - List of potential opportunities (prospects) to determine if follow up is on track
   - List of appointments for this week and last to determine additional preparation or follow up

Description of Customer Relationship Management Software Programs

Microsoft CRM
   - Adapts to your unique business model
   - The ability to modify and create forms that fit your business
   - Robust Workflow Service
   - Easy integration with Outlook
   - Robust data mining features (i.e., Advanced Find, Drill down features)
   - Marketing lists (like a group function)

Keep track of personal information, likes, dislikes, hobbies
  * Campaign feature: keep track of specific marketing campaigns

ACT!
  * Put the CRM category on the map
  * Easily integrates with Microsoft Office Suite
  * Unique, robust sales-forecasting tools and charts
  * Easy on-the-fly customizations
  * Ability to add logos and color layouts to fit your business
  * Built-in dashboard: see what need to at a glance
  * Portable: great mobile phone software
  * Group function (also has sub-groups)

Outlook
  * Easy and robust calendar capabilities
  * Easily group and organize your tasks and emails to fit your business
  * "One-stop shop": You can browse the web and navigate to CRM without switching programs
  * Hub for many ancillary programs
  * Portability
  * Has some "hidden" gem features like Notes, movable reading panes, drag and drop features
  * Color coding/Categorizing

Sales Logix
  * Built-in dashboard feature
  * Integration with back office accounting software
  * Create and track multi-channel campaigns
  * Integrated Service Alerts that help you monitor all critical business opportunities

Christmas Cards
Don't Work

Meaningful Strategies for Keeping in Touch

A s anyone who has ever been in a relationship of any kind (and that would include everyone) knows—communication is *critical*. But corresponding effectively and keeping in touch with people with whom we have or *want* to have business relationships can be especially challenging. Mass exchange of ideas is an efficient way of communicating, but it cannot and does not replace the connection made through more personal methods of interaction. When connecting with our business contacts, we need to determine whether or not this back-and-forth is 1) impersonal with general information or 2) personal and connects to the person who receives it.

Consider the following scenario:

You meet someone at a business meeting and begin an interesting conversation about the synergy between your businesses. You discuss the very real possibility of working on a few projects together in the future. You even end up talking about perhaps getting together to play golf at your club when the weather improves. You feel that the two of you have really connected, and you are excited about the opportunities that this business relationship may bring in the future.

The next day, you send an email to your new acquaintance recapping some of the conversation, and adding a few of your thoughts on working together. But instead of a response to your email, you receive an electronic newsletter from the company. You've been successfully added to his mailing list. Every week, you receive another e-newsletter, but still no personal message, even after three weeks. The connection is broken, the relationship is invalidated, and you are left disappointed. There was communication, but not any that was effective or impactful.

Great connectors and communicators would say, "I'd never do that!" And it is likely true. But this type of a situation has happened to many, including myself, and is more the norm than the alternate. Face-to-face relationships need to have follow-up. Without a systematic approach for personal communications, such follow-up can fall through the cracks of our already busy lives. It is like sending a birthday card to your mom without signing it. You sent it, but it probably has no long-term effect except a negative one. It is an attempt, but an impersonal one. And let's face it, a relationship is a relationship, and a lack of personal touch in your business connections means they really aren't true relationships—even in the business sense.

Client Communication

Right from the start, you must plan to "wow" your clients with a program of proactive personal communications that will surprise and delight them. In today's world, the more frequently you contact them, the better the relationship is likely to be. Be sure to take the following steps:

- Schedule a phone appointment
- Make a proactive phone call

- Email a client whenever you come across anything that might be of interest to them
- Invite clients to educational workshops
- Invite clients to lunch or another social meeting
- Invite clients to a meeting in your office
- Mail a personal note

Even if you have a large network, you can still break it down to a manageable number and reach out to specific people individually. Steven Burda, an employee of The Boeing Company's Financial Planning and Procurement Department, is an uber-connector. Burda has 40,000 people in his network and more than 1,200 recommendations on LinkedIn. I asked him how he possibly could stay in touch with so many contacts, and he answered, "I can't keep up with 1000s at a time . . . but 10–20 a week, no problem!! I just work to connect people together for their mutual business benefit."

Consider Personally Delivered Communications

Such as the following methods:

Video and Audio on Your Web Site

Your communication channels can also be used for educational purposes. You can include a link on your web site to video or audio podcasts that include a few minutes of interesting information about the business, industry, or clients. Then, you can inform clients through a link in an email of the video update on your site. When you are the one who is speaking to customers, you provide more personal communication—especially if the information is regularly updated—than simply writing something on your site.

Andrea Sittig-Rolf, founder of business development consulting firm Sittig Incorporated and author of three books on "The Blitz

Experience" of prospecting and business expansion, has found valuable ways to keep in touch with her Fortune 100 clients. "I prepare monthly video tips with valuable information for those that have opted in," Sittig-Rolf said. She is staying in front of her largest clients regularly and with information that she herself is personally delivering.

Conference Call or Webinar

Hosting regular conference calls or webinars on interesting information also is a way to personally stay in touch because *you* are the one presenting the message. But have you ever had a conference call dial *you*? The other night, I was sitting with my children talking before they went to bed. The phone rang. It was a recorded message informing me that if I would like, in 30 seconds, I would be placed in a live conference call with my congresswoman, Melissa Bean. Now, I know I didn't register for this call, but since I've communicated with Bean before, I'm on her contact list. I listened in, out of curiosity more than anything, to see what this was all about. It turned out to be a very interesting call to which my children and I listened on speakerphone. There were many questions coming in that the congresswoman was answering about the state of the economy and how certain things may affect us. There was even the option to press "0" and ask Bean a question (which we didn't).

Many conference call services now enable the host to launch calls by scheduling outbound phone calls to attendees. Though I would suggest getting people to register for such meetings, I rather enjoyed this opportunity. It was, after all, a polite request to listen; it gave us a chance to decline; and heck, I did listen in to the whole thing. Pique your clients' curiosity and who knows what can unfold?

Unique Events That Go "The Extra Mile"

Hosting a memorable event to which you invite clients and prospects can help build and deepen relationships. In the highly competitive public relations and communications industries, a company needs to be memorable to succeed. Strauss Radio Strategies, Inc. of Washington,

DC has found time and time again that going the extra mile in client relationships always pays off. Strauss Radio Strategies is widely regarded by both the PR industry and political insiders to be an expert on radio public relations and political communication on the radio.

"This extra mile can take many forms," said founder Richard Strauss. "I never hesitate to show a client how much they are appreciated."

Last year, for instance, the firm organized an ice cream social for a client of 13 years, TMG Strategies. They had worked on many projects for this firm's Fortune 100 clients, and wanted to show the firm and its president, Dan McGinn, how much they valued the business in a positive and memorable way. So in October 2008, they invited the entire TMG staff to a special ice cream social. The idea behind this occasion was to breathe new life into a long-standing client relationship. By spearheading a fun event for both companies to enjoy, everyone involved was reminded of *why* they worked together and how much they both benefit from the partnership.

"At the ice cream social, we greeted everyone personally at the door, welcoming old colleagues and meeting many new ones. My staff and I even helped serve banana splits from behind a full-feature ice cream bar!" Strauss said. "Later on, I invited Dan to give a short presentation. This turned out to be a great opportunity for Strauss Radio and TMG to look back on our past projects and mutual accomplishments."

The event was a great success and certainly memorable. Dozens of pictures were taken, which were later compiled into photo booklets for McGinn and his co-workers.

"Many of the TMG staffers told me they were touched, and they still bring up the event from time to time," Strauss said. "We ended 2008 on a positive note, giving TMG momentum to continue working with us in the New Year."

By going the extra mile, Strauss Radio Strategies solidified a client relationship of 13 years that will surely continue to grow.

Unique Mailings and Gifts

If staying top-of-mind awareness is a goal, sending something that is memorable is critical. Instead of just a letter to stay in touch, consider adding something to it.

Cynthia Blackwell of AOK Networking in Orlando, Fla. is a mother of six who has grown her business into a multi-million-dollar firm. Her unique connection with the firm's clients and prospects has given her an edge in the highly competitive industry of building and maintaining business computer networks. Blackwell personally delivers baked goods with a note that says, "Make it an AOK Day!" She sings "Happy Birthday" to clients, sends handwritten notes, and rarely sends email as a means of keeping in touch. She tries to do the opposite of what everyone else is doing.

CEO of Silver Spoon Personal Financial Officers Seth Greene reaches out to his clients three to four times per month simply to stay in touch. He also sends handwritten notes as well as postcards, and even has sent pearl necklaces on Valentine's Day. Perhaps the most memorable method in Greene's approach is to send letters out to his clients from his two-year-old son, Max. Sometimes Max says, "Daddy hasn't heard from you in a while," and sometimes Max asks for referrals for his dad. The letter has a recent picture of Max and is written as if he really wrote it. Response rates on Max's letter are the most successful campaign Greene holds.

Greene and his firm also host unique events (golf at Pebble Beach—from an indoor golf facility in Buffalo, NY in March!) and send out a regular newsletter with information about the firm (which make celebrities of his employees). They also mail temporary tattoos to clients featuring the company logo, requesting that customers put it on and take a picture. If they do, Greene will send a free box of chocolates. It's a lot of fun and good business as well. Greene is one of the top advisors in the country with an ever-growing practice.

Keeping in Touch through Social Media

Perhaps the most daunting task facing those of us attempting to navigate the world of social media is deciding which sites to utilize, and how active you want to be on these sites. Merely *having* a presence does not take advantage of the power of this medium. You must also:

- Make sure your profile is up-to-date on the social media sites you use.

- Post information of value to those in your network on a regular basis (daily or weekly). Pick a few contacts each day to reach out to (without selling them something).

(See Chapter 18 for a detailed account of strategies for social media).

Keeping in Touch with Prospects

The Ward Group is an advertising agency located in Dallas, TX. The firm—and the industry as a whole—has a fairly long sales cycle. Prospects are not in the market for advertising services on a regular basis, and it might be years before they decide to change agencies. "I think the longest courtship I have experienced was six years from the first point of contact to the point at which we actually did business with the client," said Rob Enright, president of The Ward Group. "After making initial contact with the decision maker and discovering the he was pleased with his agency at the time, I began a series of 'touch points.' I was unaware that this would continue for years to come."

Without ever trying to sell anything, Enright stayed in touch with this prospect through birthday cards, articles about things in the prospect's industry, research about trends in that industry, and anything else he could think of that might be of interest and/or value. "One day, I got a phone call from him and we met. Over a glass of iced tea, he assigned us his account without a competitive review or any proposal on my part. All it cost me was a glass of tea—and six years of staying in touch."

Success stories like Enright's *do* happen, but far too often we move forward without a plan and give up on staying in touch, sometimes even after just a few months. But the cost of connecting is more about time than money. The relationship existed because Enright stayed in touch with relevant information that kept him top of mind and at the forefront, and he won the business when the time for a change came.

Keeping in Touch with an Entire Group/Bringing It All Together

In 1997, Atlanta real estate specialist Michael Eastman created a group called TeamIvy (www.teamivy.com), an organization that lends itself to building on "the old boys' network" for which the Ivy League universities are famous. TeamIvy is a professional networking group in Atlanta comprised of 2,000 alums from the Ivy League universities, the seven sisters colleges, and other select schools.

Eastman has stayed in touch with his group through giving TeamIvy members quality, Ivy-related events that they can enjoy. The group hosts Business Networking Breakfasts and Luncheons with guest speakers, fund-raisers, Tables for Eight dinners, wine tastings, book signings and socials. Up to 500 members turn out every October to enjoy the fall foliage and watch experienced polo players wearing Ivy League shirts play a match at Jack Cashin's Chukkar Field in Alpharetta.

In maintaining a network like TeamIvy, Eastman touts the importance of concentrating on quality and professionalism. He spends several days a month putting together the organization's newsletter, and still more time contacting TeamIvy volunteers to line up interesting, quality, and exciting events.

"Every newsletter that I send—and every event in that newsletter—is PR and directly reflects on me," Eastman said. "It's been my security in the real estate business. Even in this economic downturn . . . I am working with eight or nine high-end clients with relatively large budgets."

In November 2008, Eastman moved TeamIvy onto Facebook. They now have a Facebook page for the organization, and some young alumni recently created a TeamIvy spinoff group "Young Ivy Plus," which also has a web site and a page on Facebook. Both Facebook groups are less than a year old and are expanding rapidly.

Eastman tries to avoid sending email messages to TeamIvy members more than once a month. However, on social networking sites like Facebook, people expect regular and informal contact. "It's really breathed new life into longstanding programs like our 12-year-old Business Networking Breakfasts. We almost doubled our attendance when we started posting the event on Facebook."

Three Types of Contact Strategies

There are three types of strategies for keeping in touch, none of which are especially difficult to implement or understand. However, when we look at those who are keeping in touch with their business relationships, they are doing these with consistency (the hardest part) and with a personal touch.

1. Meeting Follow-Up

Have a system for following up after a meeting, call, or contact with an individual or business. Follow-up may include a handwritten note, email, letter, social media contact, or phone call.

2. Periodic Individual Contact

Reach out to existing contacts on a systematic, periodic basis to stay in touch and maintain the relationship.

3. Communication Campaigns

Conduct a communication campaign to a group of contacts at one time. Schedule all of these communication activities in your CRM database program, or consider using an external Client Communication Matrix. This matrix may be a spreadsheet that is designed to organize and track your monthly communication with your top clients and can be updated and customized to fit your needs.

If you would like to access a free, download of the Red Zone Marketing worksheet, "Client Communications Matrix," go to www.redzonemarketing.com/theconnectors. Enter keycode "CONNECT" to download it for free!

CHAPTER 17

Using Speaking Skills to Develop Relationships

Simple Strategies to Connect Powerfully When Speaking to Small and Large Groups

It's not your performance or your delivery. People won't remember your gestures or what you're wearing. Unless what you say is relevant to your audience, nothing else will matter.

—Joel H. Weldon

I've had the good fortune to hear some of the best business speakers in the world through my work and as a member of the National Speakers Association, and I've observed one significant difference between some of the greats and everyone else: The most prolific speakers are able to connect with their audiences immediately, build rapport in seconds, and are able to hold this

191

connection throughout an entire presentation. They engage their audiences from beginning to end.

Those Who Speak Well Win in Business!

Those who are great communicators are able to command respect, get their ideas across more quickly, and often close more sales. They're also the ones who have developed a sense of a personal connection with those they may have never—nor will ever—personally meet. The truth is that the individuals who can speak effectively are more likely to advance through business, end up running many of the largest companies in the world, and are our political leaders.

In his book *The Exceptional Presenter*, author Timothy Koegel refers to The Corporate Recruiters Survey that is published every year by the Graduate Management Admissions Council and reported in *The Wall Street Journal*. The survey ranks business schools based on the contacts corporate recruiters have with MBA students of particular schools. These recruiters rated the students on 21 different attributes. The number one important attribute, rated as such by 89 percent of recruiters, was "Communication/Interpersonal Skills."

"People who possess exceptional communication skills maintain a distinct competitive advantage in winning new business and securing the best jobs," says Koegel, a presentation and media consultant in Washington, DC. "In an unforgiving economy their advantage becomes even more pronounced."[1]

The principles for building valuable relationships and connecting in a meaningful way with clients are the very same principles used by the great speakers who connect with their audience. The art of speaking is actually the embodiment of the connection, and a prolific speaker takes all the principles and weaves them together in a short period of time. During a presentation, the audience connects emotionally with the speaker and is ready to take some action because of the information that he or she has conveyed.

In Section II of this book, we discussed "The Red Zone Connectors Formula." The same principles apply for speaking, just in a slightly different order.

The Red Zone Connectors Formula for Speaking

1. *Important Questions to Ask That Attract Connections:* Know your audience. Ask questions in advance to find out their main concerns, challenges, internal language, and other unique elements before speaking to an audience.

2. *Develop a True "What's in It for Them" Mentality:* The underlying focus throughout an engaging and powerful presentation is to give the audience something they care about, something important to them, and/or a strong reason to care about what you're saying. Ask yourself this: "Why does this matter to my audience?"

3. *Listen! Curiously Listen:* A great speaker listens to the audience for non-verbal feedback and cues while speaking. Most of us have had the unfortunate occasion of hearing a speaker who was *not* connecting with many in the audience and didn't seem to notice or fix it. We all fall short of connecting with an audience sometimes, but when we recognize that this is happening, we need to remedy the situation by getting back to strategy #2 and develop a true "What's in It for Them" mentality *before* continuing on a path of complete audience disconnect.

4. *Get the Sale to Close Itself:* When a speaker delivers a compelling, passionate presentation, the audience will *want* to do business with that speaker—all because of the connection he or she has made with them.

5. *Create a Memorable Experience:* When a speaker truly engages an audience via stories, message, and solutions, it won't easily be forgotten. The impact some speakers can have on an audience, personally touching them from a distance, is truly unexpected.

One of the very best speakers I've had the privilege to hear isn't necessarily someone you may have heard of. He doesn't make his living earning speaking fees; in fact, he probably has never received a payment for speaking services. He speaks to get his message across and to facilitate sales for his company. He presents within his industry only, so—unless you're a financial advisor—you may have never had the pleasure of listening to Christopher Mee. Mee is a senior vice president with John Hancock Variable Annuities, and he delivers presentations regularly to audiences of financial advisors, their clients, and his colleagues.

What makes Mee such an exceptional orator is the way he manages to so eloquently connect with an audience. Whenever he speaks, he seems to carry the audience in the palm of his hands. I've seen him take an audience and literally lift them out of their seats, give inspiration and motivation, instill confidence, enlighten, give solutions, and, as a result, sell annuities without ever talking about annuities! And although some of it probably comes naturally to Mee, he works at the craft of speaking regularly. He has taken many courses, admittedly reads every book he can find on the art of speaking, and focuses on his own delivery before, during, and after every presentation.

Several years ago, at an educational conference for Raymond James in Orlando, financial advisors in attendance literally lined up to hear Mee speak. The advisors were attending breakout sessions in which, at a given time slot, they could pick from 10 different concurrent sessions. I was personally delivering a presentation later that day and was walking through the conference area to check out the room where I would speak. As I was walking through, I witnessed what other speakers would love to have happen at their presentation. There was a crowd forming in the room where Mee was scheduled to present. I looked in and saw people sitting in every available chair, sitting on the floor in the aisles, and eventually were three deep outside the door as Mee began to speak. His first words were, "I will share with you today a strategy that has generated 1 million dollars for other advisors." Certainly attention grabbing, wouldn't you say?

Design Your Presentation around Their Concerns, *Not* Your Solutions

This may sound a bit unusual, but if you can spend 70 percent of the time during a sales presentation on your client's challenges—and can relate those concerns to what you offer (with a ratio of 20 percent on solutions and 10 percent on a call to action, *in that order*)—then you'll have a well-designed presentation that will engage. A presentation—even a sales presentation—should *not* be about the speaker, but rather, about the audience. The most amazing speakers I have seen spend time getting agreement and interacting with the audience about the challenges they face, so that their prospective clients are eventually begging for solutions. An impactful presentation connects, but it *always* closes on an action.

Ask Questions to Get to Know Your Audience and Their Concerns (Before You Ever Set Foot in Front of Them)

The first thing to do before speaking to an audience is to figure out—by asking *a lot* of questions—what their 10 biggest concerns are. Even if those concerns have nothing to do with what you're offering, the more you can incorporate these concerns into your presentation and your solutions, the more impactful it will be.

List the 10 Main Concerns of Your Audience:

1. _____
2. _____
3. _____
4. _____
5. _____
6. _____
7. _____
8. _____
9. _____
10. _____

Chances are that you will be able to relate at least one or two of these to what you have to offer them and can present your product or service as a potential solution to these very concerns.

Organizing a Presentation

In building a powerful presentation, there are three distinct sections. Presentations that last anywhere from five minutes in length to an entire day can be built using this "Challenge-Solution-Call to Action" method.

1. Address the *Challenge*
2. Form Your *Solution*
3. Give the Audience a *Call to Action*

Your Opening Makes All the Difference

A first impression lasts . . . forever? If that's even partially true, the first words out of your mouth in a presentation may determine how it will connect and engage.

"I want the audience to listen from the beginning, so I try to give them a reason to pay attention." Mee says. "I'll begin with a statement that may be controversial or contrarian to their current thinking. I want to invoke a response from the audience right away."

Recently I heard Mee speak and he began with the statement, "Based on current market conditions, everyone in this room should be earning four times what they were one year ago." Now, keep in mind that this statement was made during dire economic recessionary conditions, and his audience of financial advisors were finding it difficult to remain profitably in the business at all.

"I know that prior to the presentation, some members of the audience were considering reducing staff, selling their building, working out of their house, or considering another career," Mee said. "They weren't thinking about how things are better today than they were a year ago. So, I had their attention."

The goal in a powerful opening statement is to get the audience saying to themselves, "Okay, tell me more. I'm listening. I may not believe you yet, but I'm absolutely listening."

It's a Conversation, Not a Presentation

Oftentimes, speakers will deliver a highly scripted presentation. However, some of the highest rated speakers—despite how well planned, organized, and structured their talks may appear—seem to have a *conversation* with their audience. In business, some of the most compelling communication is made to an audience of one. In fact, the most powerful presentations are authentic conversations. An experienced speaker wouldn't likely stand and deliver a formal presentation to one person. It would seem odd.

So why then, when there are many people gathered, do the principles that work seem to change? Well, perhaps they shouldn't. In front of a large group, a speaker's cadence may change as he or she morphs into a "presenter" who is performing, instead of someone connecting through a genuine exchange.

Veteran motivational humorist Lou Heckler, who has delivered thousands of keynote speeches for corporations, trade associations, and universities, also coaches other speakers. "Audiences want to believe you know more than they do about a certain topic—that's why they've come to hear you speak," Heckler says. "But they also want to feel you are, in some ways, one of them." Heckler shares that seasoned speakers apply three proven techniques when they really want to connect with their audiences.

"The Heckler Techniques" for Authentic, Conversational Speaking

Speak to an Audience of One

Regardless of whether you're speaking to 35 people or 3,500 people, use a style that feels like you're really just talking to one person. Instead of sweeping your eyes across the audience like you're an animated mannequin in a department store window, look at individuals and move from one to another with a certain amount of deliberation. Visualize that you're talking to a treasured friend.

Think of Your Talk as a Dialogue, Not a Monologue

Recognize that audience members will be reacting—even if it's sub-consciously—to everything that you say. Don't rush things. Utilize strategic pauses to give them time to consider what you've just said. Watch and observe how TV game show hosts ask the contestant a question, listen to the answer, and then pause a few moments before telling the contestant whether he or she is right or wrong. They're inviting the viewing audience to participate mentally. You can do the same thing with periodic pauses in your speech.

Use Some Rhetorical Questions

Pepper your observations in a talk with phrases like, "Isn't this something you've noticed?" or "Am I the only one who gets frustrated when . . . ?" It invites the audience members to think about what you've said and connect it to a similar experience in their lives. It makes them think, "Hey, he/she knows what I go through each day."

A Formula that Connects

Since I began this chapter with a quote from a speaker named Joel Weldon, let me tell you something about him. Joel has been one of the most sought-after and honored motivational speakers in North America for more than 30 years. In 1989, Toastmasters International (TI) presented him with its most prestigious award—the "Golden Gavel"—for "excellence in the fields of communication and leadership." Over the years, other Golden Gavel winners have included such prominent individuals as Ken Blanchard, Art Linkletter, Earl Nightingale, Walter Cronkite, and Stephen Covey. Weldon has also won TI's coveted Communication & Leadership Award, has been inducted into the National Speakers Association's Speaker Hall of Fame, and in 2006, was named a "Legend of the Speaking Profession."

Weldon's success as a speaker is the direct result of his commitment to knowing his audience, and delivering a carefully crafted message that conforms to what he calls his NFV formula. It's a simple formula, which is designed to help them:

- **N**—meet a *Need*
- **F**—overcome a *Fear*
- **V**—reinforce a *Victory*

"Your audience," he says, "isn't interested in what you're interested in *unless* you create interest and answer these questions: 'So what?' and 'Who cares?' You can do this by having an opening that draws your audience in and makes your speech topic relevant to them. There aren't too many boring topics. There are just too many boring speakers who fail to connect with their listeners!"

Weldon's proven ability to connect with his audiences and to deliver a message that meets his three-fold criteria is a direct result of careful preparation. "For every speech I give," he says, "I invest 50 hours to prepare. I know each idea presented must relate specifically to the audience. To do that takes a lot of time to get to know what they do, how they do it, and what challenges they face. Every point I'll make in my message must fit my NFV formula."

In addition, whenever Weldon's scheduled to be the closing speaker at a corporate event or convention, he doesn't simply arrive in time for his speech. "I'll have attended the entire event," he reports. "That way I've experienced what the audience has experienced, and I can be right on target with my closing message."

Having given thousands of speeches during his career, Joel Weldon is keenly aware that those who come to hear him are of one mind—WIIFM! They want to know *"What's in it for me?"*

"I realize my audiences are self-directed," he says. "I'm self-directed; we all are. That's the channel of receptivity your audience is usually tuned in to. They want to know what you have that can help them."

And providing that very help is a surefire way to connect to your audiences and to build relationships with them.

CHAPTER 18

Connecting through Social Media Technology

How to Get the Most Out of Facebook, LinkedIn, and Other Social Networking Sites

Whether you're a big established company, an individual with loyal fans, or simply someone with ideas and opinions, social media means new opportunities to create and communicate with people that care.

—commoncraft.com

S ocial media is literally exploding as a networking tool these days. These popular online technologies are increasingly coming to be accepted as mainstream business tools. More and more companies are putting their marketing resources into social media. Even Super Bowl advertisements are attempting to drive viewers to social networking sites and blogs as their call to action.

Global international accounting and consulting firm Deloitte issued a 2009 study, entitled "State of the Media Democracy," that cited the fact that people are now spending twice as much time online over the course of a week than they are watching television. What does this mean for the future of business? Well, it probably points to the fact that we need to embrace these outlets as powerful business tools. This is where customers will interact with others, brands, companies—and will discuss everything they experience. And it is certainly where your competition will be if you are not.

Social media creates marketing opportunities to engage people directly that haven't existed until now. Effective social media marketing goes beyond web traffic generation strategies; it is about connecting a message with a network of people in a contagious flow.

It's Not Traditional, but Everybody's Doing It

When you engage in social media, you have entered into a 24/7 connected community. You no longer control the message; the community does. You are now discussing the message in a free-flowing manner. It will be altered. It will be argued. It may even become beloved or, yes, hated. But by participating in the conversation, you are showing the rest of the community you are an engaged and listening member. You are connecting in a truly viral, powerful way.

In traditional marketing research, a focus group comprised of a limited number of people will extrapolate their views out to the population at large. Once the decision is made to go to market, it may be discovered too late (i.e., New Coke) that your hot idea is not actually preferred to the original version as the focus group has told you, and a public backlash is unleashed. What social media marketing affords you is a focus group numbering in the millions, ready to let you know what your product or service is doing right or wrong in their eyes at that very moment.

One of the biggest misconceptions some have of social media is that it is just a bunch of kids on the Internet. While there may be a bit of truth to that statement, the majority of social media users are either partially or fully college educated. So while they may be young, the users are not kids. In fact, users of all ages are joining at a rapid rate. For example, Facebook's demographic and statistics report showed a 276 percent growth rate in the past six months for users between 35–54 years of age.[1] That same report showed a 194.3 percent increase in the group 55 and older. With such development comes more diversity, and if you understand who is where and what they are talking about, you are in an advantageous position for your message.

The Business Happy Hour

Consider the social media conversation to be a "business happy hour." The great thing about *this* happy hour is that it is constantly going on everywhere, not constrained by location or time. Users are on social media sites at every minute of every day. Like the adage of the eighteenth century British Empire, the sun never sets . . . on the social media-sphere.

Users of social media are free to discuss any topic they find interesting and ask and answer questions with the focus always remaining on the community. It may be tempting for some to tell the virtues of their product or service, but it is vital that members of the online community come to this conclusion as a result of their own actions, and not yours. Social media requires that, regardless of what an individual has attained or achieved to this point in the real world, everyone starts off at the beginning in the social space. Each step up the social media ladder is earned by giving to the other members—whether that is in the form of a fresh, interesting piece of content of your own or by promoting someone else's content. But the underlying rule is that you *must* give to get. By adding value to the community you are making more connections and, as a result, earning more friends, more followers, and more trust.

Trust is Critical, Really Critical!

Perhaps the most crucial element in social media is trust. Trust cannot be overvalued. Social media veterans insist that users must avoid any hint of impropriety when commenting on another person's content. Any ill will or attempt to bad mouth competitors results in a lack of trust. For some, this may be one of the toughest new rules to understand. Competition and striving to be the best at the expense of others is *not* the target in social media. Rather, the focus is on relationships and the growth of quality relationships. In the end, this will have a much more positive outcome, as people are willing to speak up for and help those that they feel they truly know. *So how do you go about building trust?*

Your Consumers Will Be Co-Owners

Content creation is the single most powerful tool social media presents; it is the cornerstone in building trust and credibility. Social media's content consumers far outnumber the content creators. An individual or business can create a position with a mighty voice if resources are harnessed properly.

Encourage content consumers to work with content around your brand; permit them to mash it up and make it their own. Once they undertake these steps it becomes something very powerful: theirs! As humans, we are extremely possessive over what we deem our own. This is one of the true beauties of social media. Consumers become "co-owners" of the material and will advocate on its behalf from the highest mountain. Many organizations have already started using this to their advantage; sites like www.my.metrova lley.net afford their consumers a new sense of connection with their respective brands and promote advocacy.

The Top 10 Social Media Sites

The following will be an overview of 10 social media sites that can be effectively utilized to spread your message. Some are sites with which you may already be familiar, while others may be unknown. These 10 are among the most popular, user-friendly, and potentially lucrative locations for you and your content to be.

Facebook	Twitter
YouTube	MySpace
Flickr	Del.icio.us.
LinkedIn	Digg
Wiki	Yahoo Answers

Facebook

With 150 million active users spread across 170 different countries and territories on every continent—including Antarctica—Facebook could technically be classified as the eighth most populous country in the world, which would put it ahead of the likes of such powers as Russia and Japan.[2] Facebook started as a social networking tool primarily for college students, but eventually, the site gained traction with non-academic users, and it is now the most active social network on the Web. Think of Facebook as a social media headquarters; use it as a virtual clearinghouse. Facebook allows you to easily push your content (i.e., your blog, press releases) from various social sites.

This site is a great place to host the conversation. With 2.6 billion minutes a day spent on Facebook (factoid) a lot of discussion is transpiring here, and, as such, it makes for a great starting point for any topic you want to cover. You can almost immediately engage your audience by using your personal profile, fan pages, and the groups you have at your disposal. Facebook users designate their likes and dislikes, add applications, join groups, and attend events of interest to them, and all of this information is right there on their page for you to see.

Facebook's explosive growth has been partnered with an aggressive ad system implemented by the company that permits targeting to very specific groups. With all the data that Facebook collects about each of its users, it offers pinpoint targeting. Using Facebook's ad system ensures that your message isn't being broadcast to every member (in much the same way a billboard does), but only to those who have specifically indicated their interest in the subject. Facebook can also provide you an ad location with a high conversion rate.

Twitter

Similar in popularity to Facebook, Twitter is growing at an extremely rapid pace. According to Compete, the growth rate for Twitter is 752 percent.[3] In fact, 70 percent of all Twitter users joined in 2008, at a time when new accounts were opened at a rate of 5,000 to 10,000 per day.[4] The site restricts your postings to 140 characters; so brevity is king in the Twitterverse.

Many people use Twitter to post thought-provoking links or ask questions. When presenting content on Twitter, you must remember that it's about quality not quantity. Since you only have 140 characters to get your point across, the material you promote—not the number of words you use—is what will do all of your talking. The connections made here easily translate into business ventures. Twitter can be utilized as a platform to have direct conversations with your users, and personalizing the touch by interacting one-on-one can increase your brand's perceived engagement and increase user trust. A recent news story even told about a doctor leveraging Twitter to communicate to his patients and peers about his practice's news and updates.

Once you start a Twitter account, you may find yourself asking how to find the people you need to follow. Twitter search is the best way to seek out other users who are engaged in the conversations of interest to you and your brand. Because Twitter search is not fully integrated into the Twitter Web experience, you can use http://search.twitter.com (in fact, this once was a separate site altogether known as Summize). By typing in keywords related to your business or industry, you can quickly get a real-time glimpse into active conversations.

You might also want to visit http://twitter.grader.com and seek out some of the top users. Getting into these top users' networks will easily expand your reach. This is done by providing content that's so fascinating that they feel compelled to "Retweet" it. Their followers are expecting great links from them, and a retweet gets your name out to these followers and may even convince them to start following *you*. Twitter Grader is also useful because it breaks down the Top 50 users by city, state, region, and country. Knowing this segmentation allows you to further target your audience. A similar source of interest is Twitterholic (http://twitterholic.com), which also gives you a quick glimpse into the Top 100 twitter users.

Another approach to find power users is to look at the top blogs in your niche (Google Blog Search and Technorati can lend a helping hand). Most bloggers are also very active on Twitter. Seek out their blogs and they will most likely have a link to their Twitter profile. Start following them and use the same formula as above. This relationship could not only teach you something valuable about your market or brand, but they are also great people to have on your side when you want to push a piece of content.

YouTube

Every minute, 13 hours worth of video is uploaded to video-sharing web site YouTube.[5] It's vital that you cut through all the clutter on YouTube in order for your video to go viral. According to a measurement taken in March 2008, it would take 412.3 years to watch every second of video on the YouTube site.[6] Since visual effects are always more powerful than words, YouTube is a fantastic tool for getting your message across to your intended audience. In our increasingly fast-paced world, the way we consume information is changing, and more and more people are looking to video content to find the answers they need.

Video usage is a fun way to get informative content to users quickly. It also adds a personal touch that allows your customers to see and hear you, as opposed to simply reading your name and information about your brand. Thus, it is a great way to build trust with your users. A weekly Vlog (video blog post) uploaded from your site to YouTube can really tap into this market and, again, build trust with your users.

An added bonus for YouTube submission is that videos play a major role in Google's Universal Search algorithm, in that it gives preference to video content that is popular on YouTube and other video-sharing services. Google, in turn, presents these videos along with search results. This can increase your rankings in the search engines and provide an additional stream of traffic. YouTube videos are easily monetized if you decide to use that option; this is done by selling sponsorships and adding a short "shout-out" in the beginning or end of the video.

MySpace

MySpace's over 110 million active users worldwide spend an average of 4.4 hours on the site every month.[7] The site was a catalyst in the social media sphere, and it remains a popular location for bands, comedians, and movies to launch their latest endeavor and remain in touch with fans. So how can it work for *your* product or service?

MySpace was once the dominant player in the social media game, and would often serve as a company's or brand's social media headquarters. It served as the go-to place for all content social. Though it has since been dethroned by Facebook, not everyone realizes that yet. The best strategy is to mirror your Facebook efforts on MySpace. Although MySpace does not offer all of the same features as Facebook, many things you do on Facebook can easily be duplicated on your MySpace profile.

Flickr

The leading photo management and sharing application on the Web has also incorporated a robust social media component. You can upload content from practically any web-connected device, but the most useful is the Flickr Desktop Uploader. This application allows ease of use in posting photos online with properly placed titles, descriptions, and tags. Once you have uploaded your photos, you can place them among the groups to which you belong while using Flickr's own broadcasting service. When another user is looking for your city, the photo—regardless of what it may pertain to—appears in the feed; as a result, it gets you in front of more people.

Flickr is a great opportunity for you to get people to utilize your work and create conversation around you and your brand. By marking things you upload to Flickr as "usable" under Creative Commons with Citation, you permit other users to apply your work as long as they give you a link with proper credit. Not only can this boost any search engine ranking goals you have, but it will also create a chance for your content to start ranking for terms in Google Image Search. Google looks at the content that is around images to determine how they should be ranked, which again, creates an additional stream of traffic.[8]

Del.icio.us

Del.icio.us provides a centralized way to manage bookmarks with the online community. Users discover and share sites of interest from any computer, anywhere—not just on their own machine. The site includes networking and subscription features that enable users to keep in constant contact with people who have similar interests.

You should encourage your users to tag your content in Del.icio.us, because many people use the site just like a search engine—typing search terms in and looking for user-submitted content with those tags. Many people do this because they feel it will provide a more genuine search result because this type of search has not been manipulated: the results are a real opinion coming from a real person rather than a computer algorithm deciding upon content. In addition to raising your brand awareness, being active on Del.icio.us will improve your Yahoo! ranking for some terms, as the search engine actually uses some Del.icio.us data as a ranking factor.

LinkedIn

LinkedIn is where the Fortune 500 are online; in fact, executives representing every member of the Fortune 500 are on this site. The site population at large is growing at a new member every second,[9] and the average household income of users tops $100,000 per year.[10]

LinkedIn is a lot like a living resume. Many people will go to this site to search for a name before doing business with that person. Individuals should keep their LinkedIn profile up-to-date and not be afraid to ask others for recommendations after they have done business with a particular person or group. For many, properly managing LinkedIn profiles can act as a non-stop sales promotion of you and your brand.

Digg

Digg is the repository for all the best content the Web has to offer at that particular moment. All content is voted on by members of the community. This is the democracy of the social media network at its best. As long as the content is fun, fresh, or entertaining, the creator of that content is irrelevant in that everyone gets to see it, not just those in a particular circle. The site also maintains a dialogue so that users can discuss whatever they feel like in terms of the material on the site.

Digg is a traffic-making machine. If you can get content on its front page—or even become remotely popular—you can expect a tsunami of new visitors. However, Digg is a tricky community; they do not like to be deceived or pitched. The important thing to keep in mind for this site is to remain extremely active, read stories that interest you, vote them up, leave a comment, friend the person who submitted the content, take advantage of all the activities the site offers, and keep an eye out for others' submissions. By doing this for others, you're more likely to create a relationship that can work for you because they will vote up your content in turn as well. An entire book could be written on how to write content that works for

Digg; however, the most important thing on Digg is your network. Build a good network and become a contributing member of the community, and your content will perform well.

Wikipedia

While academia is still reluctant to accept Wiki articles as primary research sources, it has not stopped the rest of us from checking a Wikipedia page to find out what we should know about our searches. At 2.7 million, Wikipedia has more English language articles than the state of Utah has people.[11] The Wiki phenomenon has crossed over to 260 languages, covering the Earth in Wiki contributors.[12]

Wikipedia is the most popular online reference source for most people. While this can be used to your advantage, that is not to say you should deliberately vandalize an entry or use it to mislead people. That is a big foul. But if you have content that is relevant and can genuinely help people, then you should definitely find the appropriate place and add a notation or even link out. The Wikipedia community is a very protective one. You will need to earn trust and actively contribute before anything you add is considered worthy. Take your time and be helpful, and the rewards that you can reap here from being part of the "in crowd" will come in the form of unheard of traffic to your site.

Yahoo Answers

Yahoo Answers follows a pattern of ask, answer, discover. Playing on the emerging marketing aspect that people find "someone like me" more trustworthy than paid spokespeople, the site opens questions to the community at large. Built upon the collective knowledge, it has 27 different categories to place a question or review previously asked questions and answers. Twenty-six networks comprise the international component of Yahoo Answers, which serves as yet another example of the wide-reaching scope that social media offers users.

Surfers talk of the perfect wave; batters the perfect pitch. For social media, Yahoo Answers is the ideal. This is one of those perfect opportunities provided in the current social media space: the crowd-sourced question/answer site. The site provides you with an almost unlimited source of people thirsting for knowledge. Take extremely cautious steps here to not appear as a self promoter; you need to provide real and relevant content as answers to people's questions. Being helpful will not only increase your personal level of trust on the site, but it will also earn you authority, as you will be more likely to be credited as the "Answer" than an unknown user who has submitted a similar answer.[13]

The social media space is a place for genuine and transparent content. Social media is a game-changer. The *New York Times* newspaper has a daily circulation of just over one million; meanwhile, their social media presence is rising to nearly 360,000 fans on Facebook[14] and over 134,000 followers on Twitter[15]. If that is not enough to convince you, then remember this: Perhaps the most successful product launch in the world was in part made possible by social media. Our 44th president, Barack Obama, took advantage of every luxury afforded him by these social media sites. He ended up in the White House.

How can social media similarly help *you*?

CHAPTER 19

The Contrarian
Networking Strategy

Create Truly Effective Networking Not
Focused on Networking

Learning to thrive in network organizations is the biggest challenge of all. You can't rely on formal rank, position, and authority. Instead, you have to become an expert at building all sorts of cooperative, mutually beneficial relationships that span traditional boundaries, inside the company and out. You have to learn how to network smart.

—Wayne E. Baker

I n general, networking to increase sales quickly can often be a frustrating undertaking. Many businesspeople join their local chamber of commerce or business networking group, and are initially excited at the prospects. But the unfortunate reality is that it often doesn't live up to expectations; so we quit and look for another way to drive sales to our business. But wait! There are principles of networking that *do* work and that are almost opposite to what we may believe about networking.

"Giving is the greatest reward. Every day I introduce two people to someone else in my network for their benefit," said Gordie Allen, author of *Power Prospecting*. "They never forget." Now, this certainly defines the principles I've explained about connecting in the red zone—where it's not about you, it's about them. But this isn't the most common type of networking, and it may not be what we think of when we engage in these kinds of activities. And though Allen is an expert on prospecting strategies, what he said doesn't sound much like what we think of as "typical" prospecting. His strategy of giving to other professionals has allowed him to never have to travel for business again. All the business he needs is right in his backyard.

"Stop Networking!"

In his book, *Truth or Delusion?: Busting Networking's Biggest Myths*, founder of Business Network International (BNI) Ivan Misner says that when training people to network, you should start by telling them "Stop networking!" In other words, the goal isn't to be the winner of the most business cards received at an event. That just gives you more cold-prospecting and follow-up to do after an event.

BNI was founded in 1985 with the purpose of networking and referring business to and from other professionals. Today, the organization has more than 5,300 chapters throughout the world. In 2008, BNI generated 5.6 million referrals resulting in $2.3 billion worth of business for its members.

Misner notes that master networkers know that a good contact is not necessarily a good connection. "A contact is a person you know but with whom you have not yet established a strong relationship. A connection is someone who knows you and trusts you because you've taken the time to establish credibility with that person."

The focus of networking also should *not* be on gaining an immediate sale from the people you talk to. In fact, that tactic almost never works. Instead, success tends to come from focusing on building a referral relationship—one that turns into a referral connection, serving as a conduit to other customers. The goal is to build a mutually beneficial relationship with someone who may never even buy your product or service. "If your focus is the immediate sale, you're going to miss a lot of future opportunities," Misner said.

Misner refers to three specific strategies to grow a deep referral-based network.

1. *Build Quality Relationships:* Take time to deepen your relationships with referral sources. Invite them to social functions, learn their hobbies and interests, and help them pursue their personal goals.
2. *Network in New Places:* Look for new areas to find referral partners with common interests. Don't prospect right away; let the relationship mature.
3. *Focus on Others:* Adopt a "What can I do for this person?" mindset. Always give to others, and be known for this.[1]

Collaborations and Partnerships

Dov Seidman is the founder, chairman, and chief executive officer of LRN, a company that helps businesses develop ethical corporate cultures. He is also the author of *HOW: Why HOW We Do Anything Means Everything . . . in Business (and in Life)*. Seidman says, "Deeper, more lasting connections focus on collaboration and partnerships." And, although that may seem like a given truth, the fact is that most who enter into networking focus on themselves more than on the mutual benefit. In other words, they concentrate more on "What's in it for me?" than on "What can I do for *you?*"

The late American author Frederick L. Collins once made this wise observation: "Always remember that there are two types of people in the world: those who come into a room and say, 'Well, here I am,' and those who come in and say, 'Ah, there you are.'" It's those in the latter category who build friendships and relationships without even trying.

For many years, I've belonged to National Speakers Association (NSA), which was founded in 1972 by the late Cavett Robert. Robert was already an accomplished and acclaimed speaker when he launched NSA. There were few "professional" speakers at that time, but he had a strong desire to help others become better at public speaking.

In most fields, the idea of helping potential competitors hone their skills isn't a very popular concept, to say the least. But Cavett Robert would have none of it. His motto was "Don't worry about how we divide up the pie; there's enough for everybody. Let's just build a bigger pie." That bigger pie he envisioned now has 38 chapters and more than 4,000 members across the United States.

Although Robert passed away in 1997, NSA still reflects the spirit of Cavett in all its activities. At both national and chapter events, the primary focus is on members helping other members and candidates become better at their craft. From the beginning, networking has been an important ingredient. On the NSA web site, a page headed "Connection" lists the many ways in which members can build relationships with their peers as they help one another. The opening words on that page say it well: "NSA is all about connection and learning."

Networks versus Networking Organizations

Another look at networking comes from a group that actually *prohibits* any kind of selling to one another, but exchanges referrals on a regular basis. As described on its web site (www.eonetwork.org), "The Entrepreneurs' Organization (EO)—for entrepreneurs only— is a global community that enriches members' lives through direct peer-to-peer learning, connections to experts, and once-in-a-lifetime experiences. EO, an organization that I personally am a member, is the catalyst that enables entrepreneurs to learn from each other, leading to greater business success and an enriched personal life." Its members are business owners under the age of 50 who run companies that exceed $1 million (United States) in revenue. Total sales of all EO members worldwide exceed $100 billion annually.

Founded in 1987 by young, energetic entrepreneurs, EO now has more than 7,000 members in 113 chapters in 38 countries around the globe. Members come from all walks of life and lead companies of every type and size imaginable. The average member runs a company with 131 employees and annual sales of $14.4 million. Members gather because of a desire to grow their businesses and share experiences.

Shelby Scarbrough of Practical Protocol and CONEXUS Global Services in Alexandria, Virginia, is a recent past president of the Entrepreneurs' Organization. Scarbrough said, "We are a learning organization; a network, versus a networking organization. We have a strict non-solicitation policy. So we can buy from one another, but we cannot sell." The environment at EO is very conducive to forming lasting relationships built on trust and respect. "Any member would be more than willing to help another member if they can."

True to its networking mission, EO offers various programs to help its members make connections and build relationships—not only within its own ranks, but in other organizations as well. For example, its Member Exchange is an extensive database that contains the collective experience of more than 25,000 members of EO, the Young Presidents' Organization (YPO), the World Presidents' Organization (WPO) and the Chief Executives' Organization (CEO). A second program, called Meetings-in-Meetings, takes place concurrently with major trade shows and conventions around the world. It gives EO members the opportunity to network with peers in similar industries, both fellow EO members and YPO and WPO members as well.

As is the case with EO, membership in Young Presidents' Organization International is age-restricted. Candidates must submit their applications before reaching their 45th birthday. They must also have full responsibility for the operation of a qualifying corporation or division and hold one of the following titles: CEO, Board Chairman, President, Managing Director, Managing Partner, Publisher, or the equivalent of one of these titles. Founded in 1950, YPO has approximately 10,500 members and more than 25,000 alumni in more than one hundred countries. Its core mission is "to develop better leaders through education and idea exchange."

Two other organizations with close ties to YPO are the Chief Executives Organization (CEO) and the World Presidents' Organization. CEO, which was founded in 1958, represents 2,000 former YPO members who have distinguished themselves by their excellence in leadership. Membership is on an invitation-only basis. The group's stated mission is "to connect global leaders who value deep caring friendships through forum-quality, intimate, powerful experiences and relevant enriching programs." In other words, it's all about making connections and building relationships.

WPO membership is also comprised of former YPO members who, having reached the maximum YPO age of 49, move on to what has been called YPO's graduate organization. Its 4,800 members either are or have been chief executive officers of major business enterprises. WPO has more than 85 chapters in more than 70 countries.

These organizations share similar goals, among the most important of which is networking. Like the Entrepreneurs' Organization we described earlier, all are networks, but not networking organizations.

There are, of course, numerous other membership organizations in the worldwide business community that share similar objectives to those we've described. One of the oldest and largest of these is Vistage International, which was founded in 1957 as The Executive Committee (TEC). Today, Vistage and its affiliate organizations have 14,500 members in 16 countries and, based on combined revenues, comprise the largest organization for chief executives in the world. Their companies generate nearly $300 billion in annual revenues and have a combined workforce of 1.8 million employees.

Vistage members meet for a full day each month in designated groups, comprising about a dozen members each. A typical program involves an outside speaker for half the day, with the other half devoted to specific and confidential issues individual members may be facing. Each group has an experienced facilitator who also conducts one-on-one coaching and consulting sessions with each member every month.

Not long ago, Vistage launched its online Vistage Member Network™, which allows members to confidentially post questions on *any* issue and receive guidance and suggestions from the global Vistage community. Often, members who post questions receive multiple responses within hours or days. All responses are posted on the network database and are easily searchable by members.

We have many clients who are involved in Mastermind Groups, which have much the same result as these organizations I've described. The purpose of joining them is networking and sharing of ideas, and the result is a growing number of referrals.

What to Say When Someone Asks about You

I'm personally not a fan of the "elevator speech," but only because I haven't seen many successful businesspeople use this strategy. In principle, the elevator speech has merit, because it prepares you to be more concise about what it is that you do.

Well established professionals, however, seem to have a much more natural way of talking about their business, positioned in purpose, and certainly not with flash or gimmicks. In fact, when people ask you "What do you do?", they don't really want you to share for 20 minutes all about you. Just give the short version they can understand and make it exciting. Spending all sorts of time talking about you goes against the Red Zone connector principles they possess. Profitable connectors have learned to keep the conversation about the other person, yet still deliver enough to make themselves sound exciting and intriguing.

In 2001, Laura Allen and Jim Convery saw many of their friends and colleagues struggling to find work and wanted to help. While attending numerous business networking events, they noticed that many people had trouble concisely explaining what they did for a living and what they were looking for in a future opportunity. This seemed especially true for the legions of recently dislocated tech workers they encountered.

In addition, most people Laura and Jim met at these events either had no business cards or mass-produced "free" business cards which did nothing to highlight their individuality or draw attention to their unique abilities. Laura, an admitted extrovert and a fixture on the New York networking scene before, during, and after the bursting of the tech bubble, had by then honed a no-nonsense style of introducing herself and explaining what she was looking for. Jim, a database consultant with a background in psychology, was interested in identifying the essential elements of an effective pitch and creating a method others could use to improve their own pitch. One thing that was obvious to both Laura and Jim was that a good pitch had to be short; even the classic elevator pitch, typically one to two minutes in length, was clearly too long-winded for an informal introduction. In a world of ever-decreasing attention spans, less was definitely more.

What followed were several weeks of brainstorming and experimentation to identify the elements of a compelling and informative personal introduction, during which time Laura and Jim attended and hosted many networking events, putting their newfound principles into action.

Feedback on their new technique was so positive that they created a name for it and a web site to go along; the 15SecondPitch™ was born. The 15SecondPitch.com web site was launched in the fall of 2002.

The 15SecondPitch™ is a tool to help you discover who you are and what you really want. It's a way to focus your thinking on what's most important, and is a great introduction and conversation starter.

The 15SecondPitch Formula

Answer the following questions:

1. Who are you?
2. What do you do?
3. Why are you the best?
4. What's your call to action?

Laura Allen shares the following effective 15SecondPitch example:

"I'm a business expert specializing in helping companies and individuals market themselves more effectively. I'm most proud of the $5.5 million deal I closed from a cold call. In addition, Al Gore was a client during his 2000 presidential campaign. And, I once built a four-foot-tall pyramid and shipped it to George Lucas's Skywalker Ranch." Just think of the reaction you may get to this statement.

New and Better Ways

Clearly, the days of the "Lone Ranger" business leader are over. As Wayne E. Baker wrote in his book, *Networking Smart: How to Build Relationship for Personal and Organizational Success* (McGraw-Hill, Inc., 1994), "Organizations and their leaders are searching for new and better ways of surviving and thriving in the new business order." Those new and better ways include a philosophy of empowerment, instead of one of control. "Empowerment," he writes, "is the essence of networking."

Baker described the 1980s as "the crest of the cult of the deal, with its greed, avarice, and utter disregard of relationships." He then made this prediction: "Those who make it in the 1990s and beyond will take a more enlightened course. They will empower themselves and their people through networking smart, and they will turn their companies into exciting, fulfilling and vibrant networking organizations."

One doesn't have to look too far into the current business media to find example after example of organizations that are indeed thriving because they have chosen to follow that more enlightened course of empowering their people and networking smart.

Baker concludes his book with a brief quote by the late British author E.M. Forster taken from his 1910 novel *Howards End*. The book's main theme is relationships, and its motto, which Baker quotes, is simply this: "Only connect!" In my view, that pretty well sums it up.

CHAPTER 20

Coaching Your Way through to Better Relationships

A Self-Coaching Exercise for Improving Business Relationships

M any professionals have turned to coaching services to take their business skills to the next level. One coaching program offered by Jones Associates, Inc. in Boulder, CO, is based on the development of business relationship skills. The exercises and principles assist in the *evaluation and understanding of how and what* you know about your relationships in business.

What differentiates you as a businessperson is your genuine interest in sustained growth in relationships versus an interest more in transacting business, getting something done, proving something about ourselves, and then being left alone.

Creating Sustainable, Profitable Business Relationships[1]

There are three distinct stages to the process of building a business based on differentiating yourself as someone interested in long-term, mutually enjoyable relationships.

Stage One: You experience hit/miss/no growth in relationships.

Stage Two: You learn to grow relationships but cannot sustain them.

Stage Three: You differentiate yourself by the impact you leave on others, and you experience sustained growth in relationships.

FAQs

Question: "What if I'm at two or three stages at the same time?"

Answer: You are; everyone is!

Question: "If I know most of this, can I just skip ahead to really connecting in Stage Three?"

Answer: We all know this stuff; however, *we all need to go through the whole process regularly* to recognize what's fallen out, what we've missed or forgotten, and to refresh the authenticity in our relationships.

Question: "Will this really help me connect better in business and win clients for life?"

Answer: Well it certainly won't hurt! Yes, this self-evaluation has had much success with business professionals. And, yes, you will recognize some key factors that will help you build and maintain more profitable and real relationships.

Stage One: Going Beyond "The Numbers Game"

Beginning the networking process is somewhat like playing "The Numbers Game." You put yourself in front of as many people as possible, and by doing so you're more likely to meet the people with whom you'll eventually do business. In doing so, we notice that Pareto's Law applies, meaning that about 80 percent of your productivity comes from 20 percent of your relationships. If you were able to focus on only those 20 percent, you find you're actually able to increase your productivity beyond what you thought was your capacity, indeed without putting out any more effort. But how?

First of all, you need to be able to pinpoint the 20 percent that is bringing you the productivity. If you can delegate the unproductive 80 percent, you can devote your energy to enjoying more productivity in the relationships that you have. Secondly, after you've turned your full attention to the 20 percent of your relationships that make up 80 percent of your productivity, you'll notice that these people are themselves so happy with the attention they are now getting from you (now that you're no longer trying to be everything for everyone), that they *naturally* promote your products and services amongst other people like themselves. This means that your business expands beyond your current capacity.

Stage One Actions

First, notice what works and what doesn't work. Getting through Stage One requires figuring out which relationships really generate productivity and which just keep you busy. For instance, making sure you leave conversations in a powerful place is something that works to keep your space clear so you can create a future that is an improvement over the past. Leaving people confused, unsure, or otherwise disempowered doesn't work; it holds you back in the messes of the past.

Acknowledging the commonality among those moments of growth/power is the key to moving through the frustration of hit/ miss/no growth.

List Your Most Powerful Current and Potential Relationships:

_____

_____

_____

_____

_____

_____

_____

_____

_____

_____

_____

_____

_____

_____

_____

An Example of a Stage One Challenge

You're experiencing hit/miss/no growth power because of the constant barrage of interruptions, distractions, or changes characteristic of the traffic in which you're playing. The key to moving through this challenge is learning what to say yes to and what to say no to (i.e., discriminating between what is most important and then letting go of the rest).

Naturally, you want to get it all done, not miss out on anything great, do everything in your power to change things for the better, and be of assistance to as many others as possible. However, there's only so much you can do. Most possible activities will fall by the wayside, regardless how much you try to keep all those plates spinning.

Experiment with saying no to handling this problem, to helping that person, to participating in this activity, to joining that group, even just to *thinking* about something you know you can't do anything about. When you bow out of something, do so gracefully, taking full responsibility for your choice. Leave everyone around you respected, acknowledged, dignified, and completely aware of the purpose behind the choice you are making. Above all, notice which relationships most directly harmonize with your physical and mental capacities and proclivities, versus what creates stress at some level: obligations, shoulds, in-order-tos, and the like.

It's typical to think of most relationships as both urgent and important. Until you can honestly distinguish who's important to you from who isn't, you will be stressed out—guaranteed. You must take the time to observe which relationships leave you in a place of powerful peace versus disempowering stress. The stress can be in thinking about the person (worry, dread, regret, guilt, etc.) or in the physical activity of actually engaging with them (tensed muscles, headaches, illness, etc.).

FAQ: "What's the difference between saying 'no' to certain people and settling for something less than being great with everyone?"

Answer: You actually are great with everyone; you just can't see this yet. The process of growing sustainable relationships is really one that involves weeding out what is superfluous, and hence getting in-the-way of your happiness and allowing you to see that you've been great all the while. Trust the process. It's ironically the very love of life, the desire to be everything for everyone, that most gets in the way of our even entering the process of growing those relationships sustainably. When there are too many possible conversations to follow up on, you get stymied and don't realize that you do indeed "have it all." Understanding the truth in this irony means discriminating between the fluctuating barrage of conversations vying for your attention and the ones that really sustain the "you" you're meant to be. Take the first step: Single out the conversations that pull you away from those that let your heart sing.

Refining Stage One

You can refine Stage One growth in four simple ways. The point of growing at Stage One is to shift your habits from ones that are machine-like (unconscious, oblivious to your highest purpose, wasteful) and don't serve you or your purpose, to habits that do consciously serve your highest purpose.

1) Start by cleaning up and clearing out the relationship-clutter (i.e., whatever baggage is in the way of doing what's important —as contrasted with urgent—to fulfill your purpose in life through your relationships). Step away from those commitments that no longer serve you. Make room for your life's true work.

2) Create a display that shows your commitments by blocking time for them in your week. Your calendar demonstrates who you're committed to being within the time that your life provides. Displaying your time commitments allows you to get straight with yourself about what is really important and on purpose. Include revisiting number 1 regularly in your time-blocking.

3) Include clearing your mind in your time-blocking display. This is another dimension of cleaning up and clearing out, and it's to be done regularly as well: every morning and evening. It is crucial to allow the mental machinations to settle down, exhaust themselves, become calm, and leave you in the peace of your true purpose. You might purchase guided meditations to support you in this.

4) Observe whether *the way* you're being in those important relationships is "on purpose." For instance, you're doing volunteer work (fulfilling the purpose of helping others), but you're not enjoying it. The way you're going about service is self-centered, and so it's not fulfilling the intended purpose. Or perhaps you're spending more time with your best clients, trying to fulfill on the purpose of deepening those relationship, but it's not quality time, and so you're not producing the desired effect.

Stage Two: "The Relationship Game"

If Stage One is about playing The Numbers Game, then Stage Two is about playing The Relationship Game. Now the focus is on building those relationships that really matter to you more deeply, engaging more intimately in the people you want to be around and whose ways, friends, or knowledge you intend to emulate. This is where your attention needs to be if you are going to create the long-term synergy necessary to produce more than your current solo capacity. Stage Two is about distribution of material, informational and intellectual resources, and about developing mutual advocacy in relationships.

Typical Stage Two Self-Talk:

- "She doesn't respect me."
- "She doesn't support me."
- "I don't want to be a burden."
- "I've got advocates, but they don't refer me business."
- "I get lots of referrals, but it just makes me more busy."
- "I know what they want . . . "

The experience of growth and power is a matter of sustaining the relationships that support what you're up to. As social animals, the most important structures for us to pay attention to—especially if we intend to grow (materially, mentally, or spiritually)—are our relationships. You can tell you're on Stage Two in part if you know, deep inside, that it's *only* through your making sure others are doing well that you will do well.

While playing The Relationship Game, we notice that the most satisfying and productive relationships are those in which you can be yourself. You can be vulnerable, share the good, the bad, and the ugly with each other, and know that it'll only deepen your rapport because you've explicitly co-created a context for the relationship's future (e.g. "Let's open a shoe store together" or "I will refer all of my clients to you").

Stage Two Actions

First, who are potential or current advocates for you?

- You genuinely trust each other. (3 points)
- They have the kind of connections you want. (2 points)
- They have the resources to be helpful to you. (1 point)

List here the top 10 candidates for the position of advocate in your life, and rank them according to total points from the criteria above:

1. _____
2. _____
3. _____
4. _____
5. _____
6. _____
7. _____
8. _____
9. _____
10. _____

Second, tell your advocates who they are for you (now, and who they *will be* for you always). Then there's room to:

1) let them in on your intention to grow;
2) ask for feedback regarding your strengths and weaknesses (i.e. what you might work on), given that intention to grow; and
3) request they introduce you to the people they know who are themselves up for, and would grow through, being a part of your growth.

The information obtained in these exchanges is invaluable.

An Example of Stage Two Challenge

You're not really enjoying having to take all these different folks golfing, hoping they'll bring (or at least talk about) friends for you to meet/prospect. The whole thing takes too much time, you don't really like the game, and nothing's come out of it anyway. Here's the key: It's not about you; know your objective. If relationship development seems like it takes too much out of you, and they're not giving back enough, you've yet to take it out of the realm of the personal. After all, Martin Luther King, Jr. wasn't promoting himself; he was engaging the world in equality and freedom. Once you've aligned with the larger purpose your business growth serves, your (potential) advocate can look to see if her objectives are served by participating in yours.

You'll notice that an exhilaratingly peaceful energy fills you when you actually surrender to engaging likely advocates in the larger purpose that you as a force of nature serve. It's similar to the tranquility you experience when you let go of thinking and glide into "the zone" in running. You'll experience not only a sense of power, but also the appropriate results the very instant you truly let go. If you're drained by your attempts to grow, you either haven't let your guard down with people, you haven't shared authentically what's going on for you, or you haven't surrendered to a higher business purpose. It should feel invigorating!

What is your larger purpose?

_____

_____

_____

_____

_____

_____

_____

_____

_____

_____

Now call each of these people to schedule a time to sit down together.

Make a chart on which you write the times of those appointments next to their names, as well as in your calendar. Then after each interview, fill out the following form:

Figure 20.1   [Interview Feedback Form]

Advocate's Name	What I learned in the interview	Where I was challenged	Results of the interview	What's next
1				
2				
3				
4				
5				
6				
7				
8				
9				
10				

Get into these relationships. Take in what they're offering you. Listen till you disappear, until you're without reaction or judgment. Probe these people for information. If they say they trust you, for example, find out what that means to them; ask for an example of when you were being trustworthy.

Here are some additional questions to consider asking to stimulate a deeper conversation or warm up the rapport.

Possible Interview Questions
- What works for you about our business connection?
- What doesn't work for you?
- If I could improve on one thing, what would it be? What would make the biggest difference for you?
- What do you think are my top three strengths and top three weaknesses?
- Do you have any feedback, insights, or comments for me about how I can be a better referring connection for you?
- How can we work together in the future? What would you like me to commit to?

Stage Three: "The Relationship Zone"

Stage One of relationship development occurs when you notice what's working and not working with the many relationships you have, and when you make an effort to align your time around what is most productive. Stage Two takes place when you incorporate your larger purpose as your focus for developing relationships. Now let's talk about what actually sustains the growth of your purpose: namely, your ability to be the kind of person around whom growth occurs *for others*—especially for those growing into the fulfillment of their purpose(s) through participating in your purpose.

Stage Three is when you'll find yourself in The Relationship Zone. Here, we take time to *observe*—rather than be involved in—thought, the stuff of the ego-mind. So ask yourself: Who is able to observe all that thinking in my mind? Once you no longer *identify* with the thinking in your mind, you can be in the zone.

When you are trying to tough it out, get ahead, and prove yourself, living life with other people is like trying to swim upstream. Everyone resists you, and everything is hard. The world naturally opposes us when we're exhibiting our individual bundle of concerns and issues, regrets and expectations. But once you start acting from your life purpose, people start to get magnetized to you, seek you out, want to work with you, and actually promote you. Some doors open, and some close.

Give up your personal stuff. Life is so much easier outside your head.

Take a moment now to reflect or contemplate (not think, analyze, or judge) on the following:

• Fears I need to expose

_____

_____

• Ways I need to open my heart

_____

_____

• Kinds of help I need to get

_____

_____

• What is possible

_____

_____

Stage Three Actions

Stage Three is about fostering the growth of everyone and everything around you with regard to your purpose, and letting go of all thoughts or activities that would have you deviate from that purpose—thereby allowing it all to flow through you without getting hooked by your issues.

1) At which of the three stages is each of the most important relationships of your life currently?

_____

_____

_____

_____

2) What are the actions for moving through these stages?

_____

_____

_____

_____

3) What are the opportunities available to grow those relationships sustainably!

_____

_____

_____

_____

Finally, begin by living your life purpose now. This is the only
way to manifest it: Be it now in everything you do. If you were
meant to be a shoemaker, then be it fully; enjoy getting into it,
looking at the universe through it, and organizing your life around
it. If you were meant to lead the people around you, then cease
apologizing or bullying (whatever you're doing instead), and be a
true leader now, through and through.

For more information about this self-coaching exercise, go to
www.redzonemarketing.com/TheConnectors. Enter the keycode
"CONNECT."

CHAPTER 21

Financial Advisor Relationship Strategies

A Niche-Based Look at Connecting with Dramatic Sales Results

R ed Zone Marketing has worked with thousands of financial advisors and those in the financial services industry for 15 years. The following is a summary of what we have observed working right now to build small and large financial services practices using relationship-oriented strategies.

Are Financial Advisors a Commodity?

There is almost an overwhelming amount of professionals offering products and services to individuals and businesses in the insurance and financial services industry. CPAs, life and P&C agents, brokers, planners, and RIAs are all in the financial-advising business for clients. Even some unusual professionals are ending up in this industry. I was at a conference of financial advisors not too long ago, and there was a dentist there who said he was adding financial services to his practice. Really!

For clients, there seems to be an "expert" everywhere. So, how does one advisor differentiate from all the rest offering similar products and services?

I often ask advisors a few questions to determine their perceived current differentiation:

> "Why did your current clients choose you over all the other choices they had?"
>
> "What is different about the way that you do business, the advice you give, your service?"
>
> "What are your clients saying about you to others?"
>
> "What percentage of your clients gave you referrals in the last 12 months?"

Clients will tell you what your current differentiation is. And, if an increase in the client base is desired, the advisor may need to either expand their differentiation or find a way to get the word out about their firm in a new and different way. Many financial advisors have realized that if they don't create some sort of an experience around the products they are delivering, they are in danger of becoming a commodity.

The Relationship Quotient

The financial services business is, ultimately, a relationship business. The quotient is equal parts financial expertise and the ability to relate and have relationships with others. An individual looking for an advisor has so many choices that are at the same or similar firms and with the same or similar qualifications. So why does one get hired instead of another? The attribute that is truly unique to each advisor is the relationships that he or she develops, the resulting trust and confidence that is built, and the referrals that come in. Some of this industry's top advisors receive 100 or more referrals each year *without* ever directly soliciting for them. And we have seen that there is a direct correlation between the acquisition of referrals and the relationships that advisors have with their clients. The clients simply *want* to introduce their friends, family, and colleagues to the advisor.

Here are some questions we ask of even the most senior and successful financial advisors to determine their relationship quotient:

> *"Do your clients know you care? How do you know?"*
>
> *"How specifically do you show or tell them that you care?"*
>
> *"How often do you personally connect with your best clients?"*
>
> *"Do your clients like you? How do you know?"*
>
> *"What percentage of your clients gave you referrals in the last 12 months?"*

These questions certainly don't get at the core of an advisor's financial expertise, but they do quickly determine what kind of relationships they have cultivated. They are also not designed to suggest that advisors are not good at relationship skills. Most are, actually, quite good at these skills! In fact, our clients are some of the most successful advisors in the United States, and we *still* ask these questions of them specifically to assist in continuing to *improve* client connections and the cultivation of those client relationships. *It is too critical to bypass the relationship as a given or an excepted truth.*

The fact is, if a client likes their advisor, they will not leave that advisor, and they will refer more business to him or her. Performance alone seldom will bring a high number of referrals over time. And in down markets, this has become very clear. There are advisors who are receiving more referrals now than they did in *good* market conditions!

So, What's Working?

The following section describes marketing strategies that are working with some of the most successful advisors in the United States. And although many of these may be common or common sense strategies, they are without a doubt the very strategies that, when done well and with consistency, have produced valuable relationships and a higher-than-average number of referrals and sales.

1. The Client Review

Regular contact with your top clients is the key! Most advisors do hold client review meetings, but since they are so impactful for the relationship, having a systematic approach does seem to increase results and measurable success. Referrals will typically come in at an increased pace during and immediately after face-to-face meetings. So, how often do you meet each year with your top clients? Is the meeting schedule listed for each client in your database? Do you have a method for scheduling appointments that does not consume your time or your staff's time?

The Dentist Scheduling Method

One of the most successful appointment strategies we have seen is to never let a client leave your office without having the next meeting scheduled—even if that next appointment will be six months or more in the future. That's what many dentists do to keep their calendars full. And certainly, if dentists can do it, then there is no reason why financial advisors can't do the same!

Before a client leaves the office, tell (don't ask) them that you'd like to see them in three months/six months/next year. They will often respond that they can't schedule right now and will ask to call them later. But you know for a fact that when you call them later you will have trouble reaching them or they may not call back right away; the whole process can take an enormous amount of staff time. An advisor in Cleveland shares what he says to clients: "This is a very important meeting. In order to make sure consistent meetings will be held about your investments and your situation, let's get this next meeting on the calendar now. The meeting can always be moved if something comes up."

Ask them to fill out a postcard with their name and address on one side. On the other side, write the client's next appointment date and time. Keep the postcard and mail it as a reminder to the client two weeks before the appointment. Advisors have found that since the client committed to the time and date by writing their own name and address down, they will see the card—even among all their other mail—and actually keep the appointment. We work with a financial advisor who also has a business preparing over 2,000 tax returns in California each year. He schedules his tax appointments with clients one year out using this method and reports that 90 percent of the appointments stay on the books (they may move, but they stay on). One year out!

The Meeting Formula

The Red Zone Formula for Connecting (see Section II of this book) encompasses the exact strategies we have seen financial advisors use to have the most impactful meetings with clients.

1. Develop a True, "What's in It for Them" Mentality
2. Listen, Curiously Listen
3. Ask Important Questions
4. Get the Sale to Close Itself
5. Create a Memorable Experience

Most advisors are very good at reviews. But, if you can get more personal, ask more questions, listen more intently, and create an experience more than before, then the sale just seems to close—even if that result is the acquisition of referrals. The results we have seen have been significant.

2. Staff Connections

If you believe you are a great financial advisor (which I hope you do), ask yourself a question: "Does my staff think I'm a great financial advisor?" If the answer is "no" or "I'm not sure," then you may either need to work to change their opinion or they may have to go! It may sound harsh, but a staff person who is not passionate about what you do may actually be hindering your relationships and sending the wrong message to your prospects and clients. On the other hand, when they *are* passionate, then they will personally generate referrals. So if your employees don't think you're all that great, why would your clients? It's more transparent than you may think.

Hire and train staff to deliver your experience

Advisors hire staff to service and find new business, but because of very real budget and time constraints, training may not be a top priority. However, if you're going to expend the resources to employ someone, make sure their efforts are maximized and your dollars are well spent.

Tips for Working with a New Employee

1. Conduct staff orientation about the firm, the background, awards won, principles, mission and vision, rules, and expectations.

2. Explain to the new staff person all that is unique about your firm. Make sure they can repeat it back.

3. Use a "Manual Method" of training where everything that is learned is photocopied and placed in a binder so that employees can review it later. This also will become a manual for anyone who walks into this position in the future.

4. Inform new hires that client retention, new business, and referrals are ways that the firm's success is measured. Discuss your goals and your expectations of the staff person in each of these areas.

5. Give incentives! Offer bonuses for reaching individual goals as well as overall company goals.

3. Yes, Seminars Are Working!

Public Seminars/Social Events

Just when many people had written off seminars as an expensive strategy that hasn't been as successful as a few years ago, they are working again! And dramatically so!

According to advisors conducting large dinner seminars, the response rates are up—sometimes double over 2008 numbers.

"Like in past downturn years (i.e. after 9/11), we see activity levels rise with advisors placing mailing orders and in seminar attendance," said Jorge Villar, president of Response Mail Express, a seminar marketing firm in Tampa, FL. "Folks are looking for something better or different in these types of times. Consumers are looking to learn about newer options, alternate solutions, and trends."

Referral-based Seminars:

A low-risk, low-cost seminar idea that has worked in the past and continues to succeed is the niche-based referral seminar. One strategy that's currently being used is called the "5-5-5-20" seminar, wherein you simply pick five or more of your clients who are members of a particular niche (i.e., they have all retired from the same company). Mail each client five invitations to an upcoming workshop on a seminar with a topic like "How to Retire from LOCAL COMPANY in Volatile Market Conditions." Then make phone calls to the five clients personally asking them to pass those invitations along to others who are getting ready to retire from this company. Right now, this strategy is generating more than 20 people in attendance at each seminar for advisors. It costs very little (about $2 for the whole mailing), attendees are very interested in the timely and targeted information, and you don't even need to serve dinner! Advisors are conducting these seminars at community centers, libraries, and in their offices.

Many advisors have been utilizing this low-cost, effective seminar method producing qualified, targeted individuals. In fact, some have built their entire careers on this low-cost strategy.

Presentations for Existing Groups:

There has also been a recent increased interest in having financial professionals speak at meetings of groups and organizations. One advisor with whom we talked is an active member of his large Chamber of Commerce, and he has been asking for years to speak at one of the Chamber's monthly luncheons. Again and again, he was told no. But because of the heightened awareness of the financial services industry, he is seeing a new interest from groups in his community to have him speak. He went to his Chamber just recently and mentioned he had a presentation called, "What NOT to Do With Your Money Now." They bumped their previously scheduled speaker and put him on the agenda as the main speaker. Have times changed! Now, people really *do* want to hear you!

Facts About Marketing in Negative Market Conditions

Advisors and agents have tried for years to develop successful prospect-generating strategies. Some strategies have worked, and others have produced disappointing results. Today, it seems everything we've known is changing as it relates to marketing. And that's actually *good* news for those who want to grow their business!

Amidst all of the uncertainty in the market and the financial industry, financial services marketing is having seemingly unusual results. Strategies that may have experienced limited success in the past are now generating significantly more interested prospects and producing more new clients. Really! How—and why—is this happening?

The economy and the stock market are the number one story almost every day in the news. There is an elevated sense of urgency and a need for answers and advice, and investors who may have thought they had their financial situation under control are realizing that they indeed need help. People today are seeking out a trustworthy, intelligent, calming voice in all of this uncertainty that will provide an individual approach, analysis, and solutions to their financial situation. There has perhaps never been a time when advisors and agents have been needed more. In the past, advisors and agents may have had to sell services to get someone to do business. Nowadays, however, people are *looking* for you!

4. Referrals—Receiving *without Asking!*

Have you ever sat through a workshop designed to improve your referral-generating skills? Did you develop your script, role-play with others, ask yourself if you're referable, and so on? Although this exercise is of course extremely valuable for acquiring referrals, the reality is that most financial advisors would rather *not* ask, and so, this is not done with consistency. After all, most things that we don't feel comfortable doing are discontinued after a period of time. So, we will share here two proven referral-generating strategies that *don't* require asking, because ultimately, receiving recommendations is about the way you make potential clients feel and how often that happens with positive results.

Don't Miss the Boat:

One of the most successful strategies I've seen for giving clients a reason to immediately refer is an event called "Don't Miss the Boat." It's similar to a client appreciation event, but the only people invited are those clients who have referred others to your firm. Advisors say to their clients, "Mr. Client, *don't miss the boat! We're doing this big event on October 15th on the Detroit Star, that dinner boat on the Detroit River. It's going to be a gala event with music and dinner and dancing. You and you're wife can get all dressed up! But, don't miss the boat, because the only people we're inviting are those who have referred clients to us by the event date."* This event gives customers an immediate incentive to think of someone. Yes, it may be a little gimmicky, but we've *never* seen this strategy fail. It has consistently produced referrals of 40 or more per event—even from high-net-worth individuals!

The Fuel Card:

The way you say thank you to clients who refer can actually perpetuate more customers. If you send a small gift that is used *right away* by the referrer, it will prompt those same clients to give more referrals. For example, if you send a $20 fuel card as a referral thank you, when do you think a client will use it? Right away! And whom do you think they'll be thinking of when they use it? You! Most of your good clients want to recommend you to others; they may just need a friendly reminder. This fuel card provides them with an immediate reminder of you.

5. Inexpensive Grassroots-Type Initiatives

An advisor in Illinois didn't want to spend a lot of money finding new clients right now; so instead, he copied a strategy that some politicians were using. He and his staff visit the neighborhood train station during morning rush hour. They purchase coffee from the local provider, and then pass it out for free to riders boarding the train. They also give out a flyer that says, "Nervous about your investments? Call xxx-xxx-xxxx." It includes a picture of the advisor, a list of services, and their compliance information (of course!). They have already scheduled appointments, identified millions of dollars in potential, and closed a $1 million sale. It is all about exposure!

6. Your Brand Awareness

Does your brand set you apart from other advisors in the eyes of your clients and prospects? Top advisors often have a strong brand that can be described very simply: Your brand is what people say about you. Your brand is *not* your logo, your tag line, or your elevator speech; it is how someone else describes you, your firm, your staff, and your offerings. Your brand exists whether you like it or not, but you do have the power to control it.

Your Clients Will Describe Your Brand

Your clients are the leading source for answering what your firm is all about. Controlling your brand through your clients is done almost entirely through your communication. Impactful contact with your clients leads to confidence and trust. It will differentiate you from others, make your clients feel important, give them something to talk about, and bring you the referrals you deserve.

The reality is that there are hundreds of thousands of agents and advisors looking for clients. Ultimately, it will be your exposure within your target marketing that will determine your success. The stronger your brand, the more credible and visible you are, and the easier it becomes for others to do business with you

7. In the Media

Aggressive marketers are using the media to establish exposure and connect with prospects. When a newspaper, magazine, radio, or TV station quotes an advisor or prints a press release or article, credibility is increased. Let the world know about awards you've won, your charity and community involvement, your new designations or events, or your reaction to the current events or market conditions.

Once you're in the media, market your clips and coverage back to your clients and prospects. Include your press releases (whether they were printed or not) in your prospect packet. Include online links to your media coverage. Let them see your credibility!

8. *Your Community Involvement*

Being an active member of the community establishes name recognition and positive awareness. It's no coincidence that many top agents and advisors are also very active networkers in their communities. It's almost like magic, but when you give back and develop a positive brand as a good member of the community, business naturally comes your way.

9. Your Online Presence Defines You

When a prospect or client searches for you or arrives at your web site, do they see what they want to see? Does the material provided answer their questions and/or exceed their expectations? Most importantly, does it create a connection between the visitor and the financial services firm?

Seven Seconds to Make a Great First Impression

Recent statistics indicate that people form an opinion of a web site in seven seconds, and will decide within that timeframe whether to browse within your site or move on. With this in mind, it is important to have a web site design that downloads quickly, is aesthetically pleasing, and tells users right away what's in it for them. Simply put, your site needs to stop visitors in their tracks.

It's Not All about You; It's about Them!

Your web site's home page is most effective if it has a clearly stated message specifically for your target market. If you work with clients who are near or at retirement, then have a box they can click on with "Important Information To Know Before You Retire" or "Already Retired? Learn The Most Effective Income Preservation Strategies." The visitor will go toward content specifically for them. It's all about benefits, not features.

Your Site Should Be Unique, Just Like Your Firm

Having an attractive model or stock photography on your site does not tell visitors anything much about who you are. Let visitors truly get to know your firm. Powerful tools include pictures of you and your staff, video and audio (using your voice) talking to your visitors about your firm, and specific testimonials and/or commentary about the benefits you provide to your target market.

Don't Forget Your Call to Action

The success of a web site is measured by your "web conversion rate," in other words, the amount of visitors that you convert into customers. You need to nudge prospects to connect with your site so that they eventually take the action you want. Several ways to encourage their interaction is to offer them something of value in exchange for filling out information (free report or newsletter). You can also give them an option to request a complimentary retirement analysis or to schedule an appointment (and yes, they will).

Evaluate Your Site Using Analytics

Use Google Analytics tool (www.google.com/analytics) to statistically evaluate your site. Here, you can find out if people searched for your site and what key words they used. Discover how long people stayed on your site, where they went when they came your site, and if they were repeat or new visitors. Use the information to continue to improve your home page and entire site.

Financial advisors who are creating powerful relationships and connections with their clients, prospects, and communities are using these simple strategies consistently to see dramatic results. For more information on financial advisor strategies, go to www.redzonemarketing.com.

If you would like to access additional tools for financial advisors, go to www.redzonemarketing.com/TheConnectors. Enter keycode "CONNECT" to download the following tools:

1. "Action Plan Template": Organizes your marketing strategies, step by step, including the details of the project, when the project should be started, when completion is due, and who's responsible for what tasks.

2. "Client Communication Matrix": Organizes and tracks your monthly communication with your top clients. Provides suggested communication strategies and can easily be customized to fit your own needs.

NOTES

Chapter 2

1. Sternberg, Robert J., *Successful Intelligence: How Practical and Creative Intelligence Determine Success in Life* (New York, New York: Simon and Schuster, Inc.), 2007.
2. Albrecht, Karl, *Social Intelligence: The New Science of Success* (Pfeiffer), 2005.
3. Goleman, Daniel and Richard Boyatzis, "Social Intelligence and the Biology of Leadership: New Studies of the Brain Show that Leaders Can Improve Group Performance by Understanding the Biology of Empathy," *Harvard Business Review*, September, 2008.
4. Ibid.

Chapter 5

1. Tim Sanders, *The Likeability Factor: How to Boost Your L-Factor and Achieve Your Life's Dreams* (New York, New York: Random House, Inc.), 2005.

Chapter 7

1. Welch, Jack and Welch Suzy, *Winning: The Ultimate Business How-To Book*, (New York, New York: Harper Collins, Inc.), 2005.

Chapter 8

1. Walton, Sam, *Sam Walton: Made in America: My Story* (New York, New York: Bantam Books), 1992.
2. Schwantz, Randy, *How to Get Your Competition Fired (Without Saying Anything Bad about Them): Using the Wedge to Increase Your Sales* (Hoboken, New Jersey: John Wiley & Sons, Inc.), 2005.

Chapter 11

1. Colvin, Geoff, "Power: A Cooling Trend: They Don't make Powermongers Like They Used To," *Fortune Magazine*, December 11, 2007.
2. "The Hawthorne Effect," Harvard Business School, Baker Library Historical Collections.

Chapter 17

1. Koegel, Timothy, *The Exceptional Presenter*, Greenleaf Book Group Press, 2007.

Chapter 18

1. Corbett, Peter. "2009 Facebook Demographics and Statistics Report." http://www.istrategylabs.com/2009-facebook-demographics-and-statistics-report-276-growth-in-35-54-year-old-users/#more-535 (accessed February 14, 2009).
2. Facebook.com Press Room. http://www.facebook.com/press/info.php?statistics= (accessed February 14, 2009).
3. Ostrow, Adam. "Twitter's Massive 2008." http://mashable.com/2009/01/09/twitter-growth-2008/ (accessed February 16, 2009).
4. Volpe, Mike. "State of the Twitterverse-Q4 2008 Report." http://blog.hubspot.com/blog/tabid/6307/bid/4439/State-of-the-Twittersphere-Q4-2008-Report.aspx (accessed February 16, 2009).

5. Calladine, Dan. "13 Hours of Video are Uploaded to YouTube Every Minute." http://digital-stats.blogspot.com/2008/11/13-hours-of-video-are-uploaded-to_29.html (accessed February 26, 2009).

6. Wesch, Prof. "YouTube Statistics." http://mediatedcultures .net/ksudigg/?p=163 (accessed February 16, 2009).

7. Owyang, Jeremiah. "Social Network Stats." http://www.web-strategist.com/blog/2008/01/09/social-network-stats-facebook-myspace-reunion-jan-2008/ (accessed February 16, 2009).

8. Flickr Guidelines. http://flickr.com/guidelines.gne (accessed February 26, 2009).

9. LinkedIn "About Us." http://press.linkedin.com/about (accessed February 14, 2009).

10. Ricadela, Aaron. "LinkedIn Joins the Billionaires' Club." http://www.businessweek.com/technology/content/jun2008/tc20080617_789409.htm?chan=technology_technology+index+page_top+stories (accessed February 14, 2009).

11. Wikipedia Main Page. http://en.wikipedia.org/wiki/Main_Page (accessed February 26, 2009).

12. Wikipedia About. http://en.wikipedia.org/wiki/Wikipedia:About (accessed February 26, 2009).

13. Yahoo! Answers. http://answers.yahoo.com/ (accessed February 26, 2009).

14. New York Times Facebook fan page. http://www.facebook.com/nytimes?sid=ec0b3ec2e665a6e00d6ec93d1897096b&ref=s (accessed February 26, 2009).

15. New York Times Twitter page. http://twitter.com/nytimes (accessed February 26, 2009).

Chapter 19

1. Misner, Ivan, *Truth or Delusion* (Nashville, Tennessee: Thomas Nelson), 2006.

Chapter 20

1. ©Martin W. Kettelhut, PhD and Jones Associates, Inc. www .jonesassociatesinc.com.

INDEX

251